MULTICULTURAL CANADA

A TEACHERS' GUIDE TO ETHNIC STUDIES

Dean D. Wood

Curriculum Series/36

The Ontario Institute for Studies in Education

THE ONTARIO INSTITUTE FOR STUDIES IN EDUCATION has three prime functions: to conduct programs of graduate study in education, to undertake research in education, and to assist in the implementation of the findings of educational studies. The Institute is a college chartered by an Act of the Ontario Legislature in 1965. It is affiliated with the University of Toronto for graduate studies purposes.

The publications program of The Ontario Institute for Studies in Education has been established to make available information and materials arising from studies in education, to foster the spirit of critical inquiry, and to provide a forum for the exchange of ideas about education. The opinions expressed should be viewed as those of the contributors.

© The Ontario Institute for Studies in Education 1978
252 Bloor Street West, Toronto, Ontario M5S 1V6

All rights reserved. No part of this publication may be reproduced in any form without permission from the publisher, except for brief passages quoted for review purposes.

ISBN 0-7744-0175-3   Printed in Canada
1 2 3 4 5 6 TO 28 18 08 97 87

Contents

Preface/*v*

Acknowledgments/*iv*

1. **Ethnic Studies and the Social Studies Curriculum**/*1*
   Introduction/*1*
   Ethnic Studies Defined/*2*
   Ethnic Studies, Canada Studies, and the Social Studies/*2*

2. **The Focus of Ethnic Studies**/*7*
   What Is an Ethnic Group?/*7*
   Immigration/*12*
   Interethnic Relations/*19*
   The Impact of Ethnic Diversity/*25*
   What Is Canada to Become?/*27*

3. **Five Units of Curriculum and Instruction in Ethnic Studies**/*33*
   Introduction/*33*
   Unit 1/What Is an Ethnic Group?/*34*
   Unit 2/Immigration/*40*
   Unit 3/Interethnic Relations/*46*
   Unit 4/The Impact of Ethnic Diversity/*54*
   Unit 5/Should Canada Seek to Become a Truly Multicultural Bilingual Society?/*55*

4. **A Selected Bibliography of Instructional Materials**/*57*
   Introduction/*57*
   General Works/*58*
     Bibliographies/*58*; Instructional Materials/*59*; Comprehensive Works/*60*; Topics in Ethnic Studies/*62*; Immigration/*65*; Multiculturalism and Bilingualism/*69*; Ethnic Studies/*72*.
   Ethnic Groups/*75*
     Americans/*75*; Amish/*76*; Belgians/*76*; Blacks/*76*; British/*80*; Chileans/*81*; Chinese/*81*; Croats/*83*; Czechs/*84*; Danes/*84*; Doukhobors/*84*; Dutch/*85*; East Indians/*86*; English/*86*; Finns/*87*; French/*87*; Germans/*92*; Greeks/*94*; Hungarians/*94*; Hutterites/*94*; Icelanders/*95*; Indians/*96*; Inuit/*105*; Irish/*110*; Italians/*110*; Japanese/*111*; Jews/*113*; Koreans/*115*; Macedonians/*115*; Mennonites/*115*; Métis/*117*; Native Peoples/*119*; Norwegians/*122*; Orientals/*122*; Pakistanis/*123*; Poles/*123*; Portuguese/*124*; Scandinavians/*125*; Scots/*125*; Slovaks/*126*; South Asians/*126*; Swedes/*126*; Ukrainians/*127*; Vietnamese/*128*; Welsh/*129*; West Indians/*129*

Addresses/*131*

Preface

One writer has referred to multiculturalism as the catchword of the 1970s in Canada. While this is a distortion of the emphasis placed on multiculturalism, it certainly is true that many journalists, academics, educators, politicians, and members of the general public have become more sensitive to and involved with both the positive and problematic aspects of Canada's ethnic diversity.

Unfortunately, this heightened awareness has not had a major impact, with a few notable exceptions, on social studies curricula and instruction. The purpose of this book is to help teachers bridge the gap between awareness and meaningful change in social studies education and, more specifically, Canada studies.

It is my hope that this teachers' guide is a distinctive blend of the practical and theoretical, that it says not what and how to teach ethnic studies, but the all-important why as well. Therefore, it contains an orientation and rationale for ethnic studies in social studies curricula, the necessary social science background material, teaching units, and recommendations about instructional materials.

This book reflects my conviction that all these elements are an indispensable part of the process of curriculum development and instructional design. A background essay suggests what to teach but not how and why; a rationale only explores the why; a bibliography suggests instructional materials but not the *why, how*, and *what* of teaching; lastly, a unit spells out the *how* but not the *why*, and very little, for the teacher, about the *what* to teach. It is for this reason that this book provides all these elements as an integrated whole.

Ethnic studies curricula should guide students to understand and appreciate the interesting and complex features of Canada's ethnic diversity, past and present; respect their fellow Canadians, regardless of ethnic origin; and value the cultural riches inherent in our ethnic diversity. If this book helps social studies teachers to achieve these goals with students, then my purpose in writing it is fulfilled.

Acknowledgments

The origins of this book lie in a curriculum development project supported by the Edmonton Branch of the United Nations Association. That organization provided me with the resources and impetus to further explore my interest in ethnic studies curricula.

Dr. Howard Palmer constructively commented on the first draft as well as sharing his infectious dedication to ethnic studies. Dr. Jean Burnet's suggestions on chapter 2 led me, I hope, to a fuller understanding of the sociology of ethnicity.

Flora Reed of Parkland Regional Library cheerfully processed what I am sure appeared to be an almost endless series of interlibrary loan requests. Shirley Boger typed the first draft and her patience with revisions and impossible deadlines is much appreciated.

My social studies students at the Sundre School have served, over the years, as an important sounding board for my ideas about and enthusiasm for ethnic studies. Their perceptiveness and candor have been stimulating, resulting in more teachable and learnable curriculum units in chapter 3.

John Main, Ruth Sims, and Rene Salsberg of OISE's Publication Division have guided this book through the publication process with unusual patience, skill, and good nature.

Lastly, but most importantly, my greatest debt is to my wife Mary. Her assistance with typing and proofreading was enormous but in no way equals the significance of her constant support and encouragement.

CHAPTER 1

Ethnic Studies and the Social Studies Curriculum

INTRODUCTION

Educators are becoming increasingly conscious of and concerned about ethnic studies and its place in school curricula. Attitudes toward ethnic diversity are changing in Canadian society, and these changes are reflected in educational thought. In English Canada, ethnic diversity is no longer seen as a barrier to assimilating all Canadians into the English-Canadian culture. There is a growing realization that diversity enriches Canada and is an essential characteristic of our society. In addition, English Canadians are increasingly aware of the fact that many people, not just immigrants but second- or fifth-generation Canadians, prize their ethnic heritages. Following from these concerns is the belief that Canada should actively encourage the preservation and development of ethnic cultures while providing all Canadians with the opportunity to integrate into either the English- or French-Canadian societies. These changes in attitudes and social goals are both cause and effect of the federal government's multiculturalism policy, announced in 1971, and several similar provincial policies.

If integration and cultural preservation are Canada's social goals, then schools have a role to play in attaining these goals. Educators are responding to this interest in cultural pluralism as evidenced in professional journals, curriculum development projects, a flurry of professional meetings, and new textbooks and media resources. Unfortunately, to date, these activities have not produced significant changes in province-wide curricula, except in the province of Ontario.

This professional involvement with ethnic studies has generated more questions than answers and revealed that the challenges of curriculum and instruction in ethnic studies are legion. What exactly is ethnic studies? Who should be studied—immigrants, minority groups, or all ethnic groups in Canada? How does ethnic studies relate to Canada studies, social studies, and the total school program? What student goals should be established for ethnic studies units or curricula? Should ethnic studies be interdisciplinary? How should ethnic studies units and curricula be organized? What kinds of instructional materials should be used? Do these materials exist?

The purpose of this teachers' guide is to provide some answers to the kinds of questions posed above, thus assisting teachers who wish to include a study of ethnicity in their programs. This objective is approached in four ways: chapter 1—an introduction to ethnic studies, its place in Canada studies and social studies programs; chapter 2—a conceptual base for understanding the ethnic experience; chapter 3—outlines of suggested teaching units; and chapter 4—a selected bibliography of instructional materials.

ETHNIC STUDIES DEFINED

Before proceeding any further, the nature of ethnic studies must be explained, but it is first necessary to define the concept *ethnic group*. An ethnic group includes people who share a common heritage, ancestry, and sense of belonging together. These characteristics are reflected in groups such as Greeks, Scots, Amish, Chinese, and Ukrainians. A fuller elaboration of this concept can be found in chapter 2.

Ethnic studies, then, is a study of ethnic groups, the ethnic experience, and the impact of ethnicity on Canadian society and culture. The field spans the traditional boundaries of disciplines such as art, history, literature, theology, psychology, sociology, linguistics, political science, cultural anthropology, and music.[1] Some of the topics within the focus of ethnic studies are immigration history and the immigrant experience; settlement patterns; the history, culture, and social patterns of individual groups; intra- and inter-group relations; social and cultural change within a group and within society; and questions of public policy related to bilingualism, multiculturalism, immigration, and native land claims.

ETHNIC STUDIES, CANADA STUDIES, AND THE SOCIAL STUDIES

Educators are constantly being besieged with claims that some new element must be added to the existing curriculum, an already overcrowded one. The question for ethnic studies, then, revolves around why a place should be found for it and what the nature of that place should be.

The Canada Studies Foundation has identified five primary characteristics or features which have moulded Canadian society and are continuing characteristics of it. These focus on regional diversity and northern location; industrialization, technology, and urbanization; exposure to external influences; broad natural resource base; and ethnic diversity and two predominant linguistic and cultural groups. This last characteristic is expressed as "Canada is a culturally diverse, multi-ethnic country with two historically predominant linguistic and cultural groups."[2]

The Foundation developed these five characteristics in an attempt to define the scope of Canada studies and assist curriculum developers. No attempt was made to assign priorities to the characteristics. For the purposes of this book, the listing illustrates the relationship between ethnic studies and Canada studies: if Canada studies is the examination of the historical and contemporary realities, issues, and tensions associated with the above five characteristics, ethnic studies is then assigned its rightful place in the study of Canada.

Having defined ethnic studies in relation to Canada studies, it is perhaps necessary, at this point, to specify what ethnic studies is *not* as well as what it is. Ethnic studies is often seen as a program for immigrant children, or a program established to better serve the children of a particular ethnic group, or classes in the language and culture of a group for the children of that group. While these three types of programs are of major significance in a multicultural society, they each serve a different purpose and community of students and do not have the same goals as ethnic studies.

Traditionally, Canada studies curricula have focussed on only the British, French, and Native Peoples. Unless Canada studies curricula include an ethnic studies perspective, students receive an implicit message that other heritages are not worthy of consideration. Similarly, students of other ethnic origins can readily reach the conclusion that to be a "good" Canadian, they must drop all affiliation with their own heritage and assimilate into either the English- or French-Canadian community. Of course, the portrayal of any group, as will be discussed later, is as important as its inclusion in a curriculum.

Contemporary social studies education stresses the importance of utilizing the concepts, generalizations, and methodologies of the social science disciplines. Ethnic studies, because of its focus and interdisciplinary nature, provides an excellent means of accomplishing this curriculum goal. For example, major concepts such as culture, social patterns, change, prejudice, and discrimination find ready application in ethnic studies.

Values education is becoming an integral part of social studies education throughout Canada. Ethnic studies provides many opportunities for values clarification and moral reasoning, and some of these cannot be provided by other courses and units. For example, ethnic studies suggests value issues or moral dilemmas related to prejudice and discrimination, change, and intercultural understanding.

In addition, ethnic studies provides opportunities for students to develop decision-making skills, incorporating the valuing dimension, on important questions of public policy. Issues related to immigration policy, the immigrant experience, native land claims, English-French relations, and multiculturalism are of vital concern to Canada today. An emphasis on the decision-making process can include issues of personal concern as well as societal issues. Students can be encouraged to consider questions such as "How do I, at this moment, relate to my ethnic heritage?" and "How do I want to relate to my ethnic heritage?"

One objective of all social studies programs is to assist young people in understanding and relating to their fellow man at community, national, and international levels. Although the school and the social studies program cannot be solely responsible for intercultural understanding, ethnic studies can make a major contribution toward eliminating ethnocentrism, stereotypes, prejudice, and discrimination. The job can be done by giving students insight into the nature of other cultures, the impact of culture on human behavior, the impact of our culture on our perceptions, and, most importantly, cultural relativity.

What place should ethnic studies occupy within a school's curriculum? One answer to this question has suggested that

> rather than limit ethnic studies to one grade, a piece of this or that year in the total study experience, it would be wise to consider a more diffuse program whereby elements of the ethnic studies area become integrated into an ongoing student experience.[3]

Such an approach would mean that existing programs would be redesigned so that dimensions of ethnic studies would become a part of literature, social studies, and fine arts programs at various levels. It is essential to note that "elements of ethnic studies" would, under ideal conditions, be an integral part of "an ongoing student experience" in all subject areas—certainly highly desirable. However, creating such optimum conditions would require massive curriculum development efforts.

It is now possible to turn to an examination of the guiding principles which should govern the structure and scope of ethnic studies units or curricula. The concepts necessary to understand the ethnic experience are not solely the preserve of any one discipline; therefore, ethnic studies must be interdisciplinary. James Banks, the foremost American specialist in ethnic studies curricula, has identified fifty concepts from seven disciplines, which he sees as being fundamental to ethnic studies curricula. These are outlined in table 1.

In addition to being interdisciplinary, ethnic studies units must have a thematic and comparative orientation. The temptation is to select several ethnic groups and study each separately, beginning with its arrival in Canada and tracing its history to the present. This approach is not only tedious, but, more importantly, it does not provide a range of data sufficient for concept development. A thematic approach ensures that the most significant

Table 1/Social Science Concepts for Ethnic Studies Curricula

Discipline	Key Concepts	Discipline	Key Concepts
Anthropology	culture culture diversity acculturation forced acculturation cultural assimilation race racial mixture sub-culture syncretism melting pot cultural genocide ethnocentrism	Political Science	power powerless separatism oppression social protest interest group legitimacy authority power elite colony colonized rebellion
Economics	scarcity poverty production consumption capitalism economic exploitation	Psychology	identity aggression repression displacement
Geography	ethnic enclave region ghetto inner-city location	Sociology	discrimination ethnic group ethnic minority group prejudice racism socialization status values
History	immigration migration change		

Note: James Banks, "Teaching for Ethnic Literacy: A Comprehensive Approach," *Social Education*, vol. 37, no. 8, 1973, p. 749.

aspects of the ethnic experience are examined and the themes, selected from the conceptual framework of ethnic studies, are guides to inquiry. Some examples of such themes are social and cultural change among ethnic groups, immigration history, the immigrant experience, and interethnic relations. The comparative orientation facilitates concept development as well as providing insights into the diversity of experiences encountered by various ethnic groups in Canada.

Coupled with the above emphasis, carefully designed criteria are needed to select which groups to include in any unit or curriculum. Obviously, students can not study the culture and immigrant experience of all groups; therefore, their learnings are affected by their teachers' choices. Too often only the groups that are highly visible because of physical or cultural differences are selected. This is understandable because instructional materials are most readily available on minority groups, such groups can be readily identified, and there is a widespread curiosity about peoples such as the Hutterites or the Inuit. However, this presents only one facet of the ethnic experience, and students can come to see ethnicity through a false perspective.

To fully reflect the ethnic experience in Canada, information about many and different ethnic groups must be used as instructional content. It is obvious that a study of the concept *assimilation* in relation to Germans in Canada would lead students to quite different conclusions than would such a study in relation to Indians and Métis. If these three groups and several others, each reflecting a different experience, were used as instructional content, then a more balanced concept would emerge.

Ethnic studies must represent many groups regardless of the ethnic composition of the community or classroom. If such factors determined the content of ethnic studies, students in Baddeck, Nova Scotia, would study primarily the Scots and students in Toronto would study a great number of groups. Obviously, both sets of students would gain a false impression of ethnicity in Canada. However, a study of the local community is an effective starting point for comparative studies.

Too often ethnic studies is thought of in terms of folk festivals, Christmas customs, fancy costumes, and great men. Emphasis on an interdisciplinary, social science-based approach, as stressed here, should lead to a more comprehensive and more realistic approach. Ethnic studies in the schools must avoid

> entanglements in filial-pietous generalities—wise men, heroes, great events, and an unending series of contributions. The controversies, tensions, and frictions that have characterized the history of ethnicity and pluralism in Canada must be recognized and honestly approached. It must not be hidden under layers of brotherhood rhetoric and folk music.[4]

Ethnic studies must stress the human experience. This is almost a truism, but, unless a conscious effort is made to focus on this dimension, it can easily be ignored. For example, rather than studying immigration exclusively in terms of time periods, attitudes, statistics, and settlement patterns, students should be challenged to consider the immigrants' experiences on a sailing ship, their difficulties with a new language, and their isolation from their families and all things familiar.

One way to accomplish this is by letting the group speak. This includes searching out resource people, appropriate media resources, or writings by group members reflecting the ethnic experience of that group. In this way students receive a more meaningful and stimulating exposure to the culture and experiences of their fellow Canadians.

Ethnic studies curricula must recognize the diversity, which is characteristic to varying degrees, of all ethnic groups. If we teach that Chinese and Jewish children are excellent students because their cultures value academic achievement, we run the risk of creating new stereotypes as the by-product of the search for new understandings. Such a statement implies that all young people in both cultures have been socialized in the same way and have accepted the same values. Differences within ethnic groups can result from age, sex, level of education, length of residence in Canada, and variations in degrees of assimilation.

Finally, it must be emphasized that ethnic studies should stress the similarities which unite people despite differences in race or culture. James Banks has said that the

> emphasis in ethnic studies should be on the human characteristics and values of ethnic groups, and not on strange customs or tangible cultural elements like teepees and sombreros. Ethnic content should be used to help students learn that all human beings have common needs and characteristics, although the ways in which these traits are manifested differ cross-culturally.[5]

Such an emphasis will ensure that ethnic studies curricula do, in fact, open doors to greater understanding and self-awareness.

Notes

1. Cornelius J. Jaenen, "Ethnic Studies: An Integral Part of Canadian Studies," in *Identities: The Impact of Ethnicity on Canadian Society*, ed. Wsevolod W. Isajiw (Toronto: Peter Martin Associates, 1977), p. xi.

2. A. B. Hodgetts and Paul Gallagher, *Teaching Canada for the '80s* (Toronto: Ontario Institute for Studies in Education, 1978), pp. 11-12.

3. Howard Palmer and Harold Troper, "Canadian Ethnic Studies: Historical Perspectives and Contemporary Implications," *Interchange*, vol. 4, no. 4, 1973, p. 22.

4. Palmer and Troper, "Canadian Ethnic Studies," p. 22.

5. James Banks, "Ethnic Studies as a Process of Curriculum Reform." Address delivered to Pluralism in a Democratic Society Conference, Anti-Defamation League of B'nai B'rith, New York, April 1975, p. 6.

CHAPTER 2

The Focus of Ethnic Studies

This chapter explores some of the social science concepts which are central to the field of ethnic studies. The purpose of the chapter is, first, to provide teachers with an understanding of the relevant concepts and, second, to serve as a basis for the units of curriculum and instruction in chapter 3. This survey is an introduction to a complex field which spans several disciplines. The references cited at the end of this chapter and in the ethnic studies section of the bibliography in chapter 4 provide the starting point for a comprehensive perusal of the literature.

WHAT IS AN ETHNIC GROUP?

There are twelve concepts which are fundamental to an understanding of this chapter. These are ethnic group, ethnic identity, ethnic origin, race, nationality, immigrant, charter group, Anglophone, Francophone, English-Canadian community, French-Canadian community, and ethnic minority group.

KEY CONCEPTS
Definitions of ethnic group vary, but most include some or all of the following elements:

1. shared culture and social patterns
2. ethnic identity or a sense of peoplehood
3. significant interaction by group members with other group members outside the family
4. descent from people with a similar ancestry
5. recognition of individuals' group membership by non-members[1]

Different authors stress or omit different elements according to their perspectives; however, ethnic identity is usually given predominance in recent Canadian definitions.

Because the meanings attached to this concept vary in both popular usage and the social sciences, it is necessary to establish a working definition before proceeding any further. Most importantly, an ethnic group shares an identity or a sense of peoplehood. Because of their emotional commitment or sense of belonging to an ethnic group, people set themselves apart from other people and create a solidarity with others of similar sentiments and backgrounds. Group members either share significant cultural patterns (e.g. values and norms) and social patterns (e.g. roles and socialization practices) or are descended from people who did. A shared ethnic origin, the group membership of one's ancestors, sets an ethnic group apart from other groups that share distinctive cultural patterns and identities—for example, hippies and members of religious communes.[2] The remaining two elements—significant interaction and recognition of group membership—of the five stated above are also being included in this definition.

Because of the significance of ethnic identity, it is important to offer several additional comments about it. As a result of group members' self-definition, they become defined as members of a particular group by people who belong to other groups. Thus, group membership becomes a matter of both self-definition and definition by non-group members. Members of visible minorities, such as Blacks and South Asians, are frequently assumed to belong to particular ethnic groups, based on their physical characteristics, regardless of their own self-definitions.

Identification with an ethnic group can arise from one of two sources. First, it can result from primary socialization in the culture of a particular group and then retaining the culture and identification throughout adulthood. The second source of identification lies in the choices made by

> people who are descendants of those who share a distinct culture, but have gone through the primary process of socialization partially or totally in a different culture. The main link that binds these people to the ancestral group is not the sharing of its culture; rather, it is a feeling of identity with them. This identity may take various forms and degrees . . .[3]

Obviously it is not possible to delineate precise distinctions between the two sources of ethnic identification. However, this perspective facilitates an understanding of people who identify with an ethnic group but are not part of a distinctive culture in any significant way.

It must be remembered that an individual's ethnic identity is fluid, rather than being static over time and unrelated to the person's life situation. In a particular context, one might define oneself as a French Canadian in relation to English Canadians; or as a Franco-Ontarian in relation to Québécois or WASP Ontarians; or as a Canadian in relation to Americans. The specificity of an individual's self-definition can vary in relation to the commitments operating in a situation. Obviously, one's ethnic identity can also vary in relation to highly personal considerations such as age, education, place of residence, and occupation.[4]

It is incorrect to assume that the concepts *ethnic group* and *nationality* are synonymous. Nationality refers to a person's citizenship, which can be very different from his ethnic group membership. For example, the Oklahoma Blacks who arrived in the West around 1910 were American citizens but at the same time were members of a distinctive ethnic group.

Similarly, it is equally incorrect to assume that the concepts *ethnic group* and *immigrant group* are synonymous. Immigrants are people who were born in another country and are now making their home in Canada. They are usually members of their ethnic group, be it Scottish, Ukrainian, or West Indian. Immigrants often are the most visible members of an ethnic group because of their use of the native language, and/or greater attachment to ethnic customs or dress, but their Canadian-born children and grandchildren may also identify with the ethnic group.

It was common during the early twentieth century to regard ethnic groups as racial groups. The tendency was to include not only physical but social and cultural characteristics as part of the concept of race; as a result, social and cultural differences among ethnic groups were seen as the product of inheritance, not learning. Physical anthropologists and biologists now define race exclusively in terms of physical characteristics. The division of mankind into three major races—Negroid, Mongoloid, and Caucasoid—is the result of using criteria

> based essentially on physical characteristics of size, the shape of the head, eyes, ears, lips, and nose, and the color of skin and eyes. The hereditary characteristics, such as skin color

(widely used as a criterion of race), are not exclusive to any racial group, but rather overlap from one racial category to another. The characteristics used in classification are determined on a statistical basis, that is, according to frequency of occurrence, with a higher percent of certain characteristics in each classification.[5]

At present the concept of race is receiving greater currency as a result of growing discrimination directed against non-white ethnic groups in Canada's major cities. In fact, most of the characteristics of the victims which inflame the prejudiced are not racial characteristics but ethnic characteristics: language, dress, social behavior, food, hair styles, and family patterns. However, without real or supposed racial characteristics, it would be much more difficult for the prejudiced to single out their victims and identify them as an out-group.

A *charter group* is the first ethnic group to establish effective control (according to the frame of reference of European cultures) over a territory, subduing native peoples, if necessary, in the process.[6] Canada's charter groups, the British and French, have retained varying degrees of dominance over the institutions and social and cultural patterns of Canadian society and have determined who could enter Canada. This is not to say that the two charter groups in Canada have had equal power or have always agreed on who should enter the country.

The concepts of Anglophone and Francophone, referring to the two linguistic communities in Canada, are closely related to the concept of charter group. Usage of these concepts varies; sometimes their meaning is expanded to include cultural and social characteristics. In this context, the very specific meaning of language use will be used: Canadians who communicate with the larger society in English are Anglophones and Canadians who communicate in French are Francophones.

Two distinct and dominant communites—English-Canadian and French-Canadian—have emerged from the charter groups. The cultural and social patterns of these communities have their origins in their British and French heritages. Factors such as Americanization, industrialization, urbanization, and immigration have resulted in these two communities developing distinctive characteristics resulting from their Canadian experience. These communities are today, then, different from each other and different from the contemporary cultural and social patterns of Great Britain and France.

Most of the members of the English- and French-Canadian communities, especially in the case of French Canadians, are of British and French origin respectively. However, these two communities include Canadians of other ethnic origins who have been socialized or assimilated into either community. Such persons may know their ethnic origin but don't associate or identify with the group of their origin.

Again usage varies, but these communities are not being defined here as ethnic groups because of the diversity of ethnic origins, cultural patterns, and identities which exist within each community. This does not preclude, however, the existence of ethnic groups such as the Welsh or Scottish as entities separate from the English-Canadian community. Similarly, such a definition of the French-Canadian community does not invalidate referring to the Québécois, Franco-Manitobans, or Acadians as ethnic groups.

It is helpful to distinguish between an *ethnic group* and an *ethnic minority group*. An ethnic minority group is set apart from the larger society because of its physical, social, or cultural characteristics and is accorded unequal treatment and opportunities.[7] Louis Wirth, a sociologist, has provided an excellent summary of the attributes of an ethnic minority group.[8] The ethnic minority group is held in low esteem, and those characteristics which set it apart are similarly accorded low status. Members of such a group are usually socially isolated and can be separated residentially. The group experiences a relatively disadvantaged social, economic, and political position; hence, members have unequal access to educational and occupational opportunities and advancement. Consequently, individuals face greater than average degrees of economic and social insecurity and individual development is frustrated. Minority status sometimes results in minorities receiving unequal protection and rights in terms of the law and government policies.

ETHNIC CULTURES

The initial definition of an ethnic group included a distinctive culture as one of its fundamental characteristics. In general terms, culture is made up of patterns or ways of acting, thinking, feeling, and believing. People, living together in groups or societies, have created cultures over the centuries and these cultures have been transmitted from generation to generation. Ethnic cultures should be studied in their Canadian context, bearing in mind that they are not necessarily a duplicate of the culture in the groups' native lands. These cultures, after their transplant to Canada, become separate entities, changing with time and varying in degrees of heterogeneity.

Often ethnic cultures are thought of almost exclusively in terms of foods, dress, and folk arts. While these are important, such a definition omits values, norms, beliefs, and language—those cultural attributes which mould people's perceptions and their relationships with each other and the world around them. A more balanced perspective on culture emerges by thinking of it in terms of its non-material and material components.

Non-material culture consists of

> prescribed ways of behaving or norms of conduct, beliefs, values, and skills, along with the behavioral patterns and uniformities based on these categories.[9]

Material culture consists of "the artifacts created by these skills and values...."[10] For example, the churches the Amish build—material culture—are a product of the skills of their non-material culture, and the style of building they use is heavily influenced by their religious beliefs—non-material culture.

One of the best explanations of non-material culture states that:

> Among the people in each group there are common understandings concerning the meaning of various objects and the proper ways in which they are to be handled. There are shared values—conceptions of what is beautiful or ugly, good or bad, desirable or undesirable. There are numerous norms of conduct—how various categories of people are to be approached and what may or may not be done with reference to them. Culture consists of the assumptions with which people in a particular group approach their world, assumptions that are learned by each new generation while participating in organized transactions. Because they have similar orientations toward their environment, men who share a common culture develop similar behavior patterns.[11]

These non-material aspects of a culture are seldom stated explicitly and only rarely are they explained or discussed among group members or among groups.

For people who have been socialized in an ethnic culture it is the non-material aspects of culture, the common understandings, values, and norms of conduct, which shape their lives. Through such socialization they learn how to relate to kin, friends, and those outside their group. They also learn a concept of who they are—their identity—and how to perceive the natural and man-made environments around them. Similarly, members of an ethnic culture develop distinctive perspectives on man's destiny and what constitutes the "good life."

Intercultural understanding is best achieved by appreciating a group's non-material culture. Enjoyment of, and/or participation in, a group's songs and dances provides only a limited insight into the day-to-day life of a culture. In addition, focussing on the non-material aspects of an ethnic culture reveals them to be dynamic and ongoing entities rather than static museums of folk arts imported from the home country.

The material aspects of a culture, especially the folk arts, provide a focal point for people who have been socialized primarily in another culture but who wish to identify with their ethnic heritage. To such ethnic rediscoverers the folk arts are symbols of their heritage, or roots; hence, their participation in such activities is an expression of their self-identification.

The lack of attention paid to language in this discussion of culture so far does not imply that it is of little importance. Obviously the language of an ethnic group makes communication possible among group members and, at least among the first and second generations, serves as the mechanism for transmitting culture. The decline in usage of the ethnic language does not necessarily mean that the culture is dying or losing its significance. A. P. Campbell, reflecting on his ethnic experience as a member of the Highland Scots of Prince Edward Island during the 1910s and 1920s, said that although Gaelic was rarely used, the culture was very much alive among the people.[12] On the other hand, most ethnic leaders see a direct relationship between the survival of the language and the ongoing vitality of the culture. Without knowledge of a group's language it is very difficult (many say impossible) to understand its folk arts or, more importantly, the nuances of its non-material culture.

ETHNIC SOCIAL PATTERNS

An ethnic group, as well as being characterized by a distinctive culture, is the possessor of equally distinctive social patterns. A study of a group's social patterns includes topics such as marriage and the family, social classes, interpersonal relationships, urban and rural lifestyles, social control, religious activities, political participation, voluntary associations, and education. This present discussion will be limited to an examination of marriage and the family, interpersonal relationships, voluntary associations, religion, and education.

Marriage and the family can be examined by studying the kinship bonds characteristic of an ethnic group. What are these bonds, how strong are they, and what are the responsibilities associated with them? Does the family include only the parents and their offspring—the nuclear family—or does it include various relatives of the parents—the extended family? There are roles for each of the social positions—for example, grandparent, mother, uncle, child, young adult—within the family. These roles basically are rules that spell out the behaviors and expectations accompanying each social position. The degree of ethnic endogamy—marrying within the group—as opposed to ethnic exogamy—marrying outside the group—is an important indicator of "the extent to which they [group members] are still bound by their cultural heritages and social networks."[13] The family should also be examined in the light of its role as a socializing agent. Does the family seek to socialize its children into the distinctive cultural and social patterns of that group? Conflict often arises within the family and between the family and other socializing agents, such as the school, because those agents are controlled by the larger society and often represent different social and cultural patterns.

Interpersonal relationships are best thought of in terms of primary and secondary relationships. Personal friendships, home intervisiting, group worship, and group recreation characterize primary relationships. Secondary relationships are those associated with earning a living, carrying out political responsibilities, and group activities in the larger community.[14] When studying the primary and secondary relationships of group members, it is important to determine the extent to which these relationships take place within the group in contrast to relationships with non-group members. The extent to which interpersonal relationships take place within the group is an important indicator of the degree of assimilation, integration, or both.

The primary relationships of ethnic group members are influenced by the institutional completeness of their group. An institutionally complete ethnic group can provide all the services its members need: educational facilities; churches and religious organizations; stores and restaurants; professional services by doctors and lawyers; and voluntary associations.[15] This concept is best understood in terms of a continuum, ranging from groups which provide few services for themselves to groups which are almost completely self-sufficient.

One research study found a direct and significant relationship between the degree of institutional completeness characteristic of a group and the proportion of immigrant members' primary relationships within the group.[16] It is probable that there is a similar relationship between institutional completeness and the primary relationships of non-immigrant members of an ethnic group.

Voluntary associations. The organizational facet of a group's social life is revealed by an examination of its voluntary associations, such as material aid associations, women's groups, immigrant aid societies, political organizations, youth groups, and social, athletic, and cultural associations. What associations exist and for what purpose? How active are group members in these associations? Is the purpose of the association changing with time? Do the associations reveal social, educational, and economic differences within the group?

Research shows that a group with a large percentage of ethnically exclusive organizations is less likely to be socially integrated with the larger society than a group with relatively few exclusive organizations. As a general rule, ethnic groups that see their origin as a disadvantage establish numerous and strong associations, whereas ethnic groups (e.g. the Dutch) that share a cultural affinity with English Canadians and have faced few barriers in Canada establish comparatively few associations. Individuals who are active participants in these associations tend to have a strong sense of ethnic identity.[17]

Religion. Religious institutions serve to maintain ethnic culture and a sense of ethnic identity, especially for groups such as Jews and Mennonites. Many ethnic groups have established either their own churches in Canada or parishes or congregations of existing Canadian churches using the language of the group. The desire to use the familiar language in religious activities has led churches to play an important role in language instruction.

Education. In the area of education an ethnic group can be studied in terms of its educational achievement and aspirations. The most meaningful area of study, however, is the interaction of the culture and social patterns of either the English- or French-Canadian community, as presented by the educational system, with that of the ethnic group. What impact does education in one of the official languages have on children's knowledge and appreciation of their mother tongue? Are the values, norms, and roles taught and/or reflected by the school system supportive of or in conflict with those taught at home? Does conflict occur in the home as the result of the child becoming increasingly bicultural?

Many ethnic groups establish part-time schools to train their children in the language, culture, and religion of their forefathers. These schools "contribute to a feeling of cultural identity on the part of those who attend by teaching them the language and culture of their parents, as well as by setting them apart from other children."[18]

IMMIGRATION

Quite obviously our multicultural society is the product of immigration. Because Canada's immigrants have come from increasingly diverse sources, especially since the 1960s, Canadian society has been transformed from its essentially bicultural character of 1867. In addition to studying immigration for this reason, it is important to examine the public policy dimension of immigration. The debate generated by the Green Paper (1975), the Special Joint Committee of the Senate and the House of Commons on Immigration Policy (1975), and the Immigration Act (1976) provides ample evidence that Canadians are concerned about immigration, hold varying and often conflicting opinions about desirable policy, and see immigration as an important factor influencing many facets of our society. The reception accorded to immigrants and their experiences in this country reveal much about Canadian society past and present. Because all Canadians, except the Native Peoples, are either descendants of immigrants or immigrants themselves, a study of immigration becomes a study of our heritage.*

MOTIVATIONS FOR IMMIGRATION

The motivations of the immigrants who have arrived on Canada's doorstep have been many and varied. These should be examined from the perspective of conditions in both the sending and receiving countries as well as the aspirations of individuals.

People have chosen to immigrate to Canada because they anticipate significant economic advantages, as illustrated by the flow of immigrants from Portugal and Italy in recent years. The decline in the numbers of West Germans entering Canada is explained by the upsurge in prosperity in the home country. Economic disasters in the sending country, such as the Irish Potato Famine, or the effects of World War II on Germany, stimulate immigration.

Political conditions in the sending and receiving countries are also of enormous importance. Canada has opened its doors to thousands of refugees fleeing political systems or situations they regarded as undesirable or dangerous to their well-being. Refugee groups such as the Chileans, Hungarians, and Ugandan Asians have fled totalitarian regimes, or have sought new homelands after being expelled from their own country. Canada's democratic political system and stable political history have been attractions drawing immigrants to Canada. In addition, government policies, a product of Canada's political system, play a significant part in determining whether Canada is seen as an attractive place to settle. Such policies determine whether immigrants will be actively sought by establishing offices in foreign countries, offering inducements such as land grants and travel aid, and providing resettlement assistance upon arrival in Canada.

The desire for religious and cultural freedom has encouraged immigrants to seek a home in Canada. The Hutterites and Doukhobors have entered Canada seeking religious freedom and, in the broader sense, freedom to preserve and maintain their culture unimpeded by outside pressures.

Not all immigrants have entered Canada because of economic, political, or religious reasons. The desire to travel, freedom from the constraints of family and/or a traditional society, greater educational opportunities, and failure to gain entrance to another country all have an important impact on the decision to immigrate to Canada.

IMMIGRATION HISTORY

Canadian immigration history since Confederation can be broken down into four major periods: 1867 to 1896, 1896 to the outbreak of World War I, the interwar years, and the post-World War II era. Each of these will be examined briefly with a view to outlining the trends characteristic of the period.[19]

The 1871 census revealed that only 8 per cent of Canada's population was of non-British, non-French ethnic origin. The Germans constituted the only other ethnic origin category of any significant size. In contrast, as illustrated in table 2, the 1971 census revealed that this 8 per cent had grown to 26 per cent. More dramatically, the 1971 census figures indicated that 43 per cent of Metropolitan Toronto's population was of non-British, non-French origin; the corresponding figure for the province of Alberta was 47 per cent.

During the first phase little change took place in the ethnic composition of Canada. Immigration served to reinforce existing patterns as evidenced by the 1901 census, which showed that the non-charter group population made up only about 10 per cent of the

---

*On occasion Indians and Inuit have been referred to as Canada's first immigrants, thus carrying the definition of immigrant to the point of absurdity.

Table 2/Ethnic Origin of the Canadian Population (percentages), 1871-1971

	1871	1881	1901	1911	1921	1931	1941	1951	1961	1971
Total	100.00	100.00	100.00	100.00	100.00	100.00	100.00	100.00	100.00	100.00
British	60.55	58.93	57.04	55.49	55.41	51.86	49.68	47.89	43.85	44.6
French	31.07	30.03	30.71	28.61	27.91	28.22	30.27	30.83	30.38	28.7
Dutch	0.85	0.70	0.63	0.78	1.34	1.44	1.85	1.89	2.36	2.0
German	5.82	5.88	5.78	5.60	3.35	4.56	4.04	4.43	5.75	6.1
Italian	0.03	0.04	0.20	0.64	0.76	0.95	0.98	1.09	2.47	3.4
Jewish	*	0.02	0.30	1.06	1.44	1.51	1.48	1.30	0.95	1.4
Polish			0.12	0.47	0.61	1.40	1.45	1.57	1.77	1.5
Russian	0.02	0.03	0.37	0.61	1.14	0.85	0.73	0.65	0.65	0.3
Scandinavian	0.05	0.12	0.58	1.56	1.90	2.20	2.12	2.02	2.12	1.8
Ukrainian			0.10	1.05	1.21	2.17	2.66	2.82	2.59	2.7
Other European	0.11	0.13	0.44	1.35	2.44	2.51	2.45	2.47	3.90	3.9
Asiatic	*	0.10	0.44	0.60	0.75	0.81	0.64	0.52	0.67	1.3
Indian and Eskimo	0.66	2.51	2.38	1.46	1.29	1.24	1.09	1.18	1.21	1.4
Others and Not Stated	0.84	1.51	0.91	0.72	0.45	0.28	0.56	1.34	1.33	1.0

*Percentage lower than 0.01

Source: Canada. Royal Commission on Bilingualism and Biculturalism. *Report of the Royal Commission on Bilingualism and Biculturalism: Book IV The Cultural Contribution of the Other Ethnic Groups* (Ottawa: Information Canada, 1970), p. 248 and Census of Canada, 1971, Catalogue 92-723.

population. Of the immigrants entering the country, over half were German. Emigration was a major characteristic of this era; it is estimated that more people left the country during each decade from 1861 to 1901 than entered it. In 1896, when Clifford Sifton assumed the responsibility for immigration, only three classes of people were prohibited entry into Canada—the diseased, the criminal or vicious, and those likely to become public charges.[20]

The second phase is the well-known immigration period that resulted in the settling of the West. Between 1896 and 1914, as the result of a policy initiated by Prime Minister Laurier's government, three million immigrants entered Canada. In 1913, 400 000 people entered Canada, the largest number ever recorded. Of the three million immigrants who entered Canada at this time, only 1 250 000 were from the United Kingdom, and about one million were from the United States. Thus, this period is distinctive for more than sheer numbers; new sources of immigrants were appearing. It has been said of this period that "the outstanding feature . . . was the influx of immigrants from central and eastern Europe—Ukrainians, Poles, Hungarians, Roumanians, and Russians."[21]

In this period, Canada imposed its first restrictions directed against particular ethnic groups. A "head tax" was implemented to limit Chinese immigration, and a "gentlemen's agreement" was created with Japan by which that country agreed to limit the emigration of laborers. Regulations established in 1908 requiring immigrants to travel to Canada by a continuous voyage from their home country almost completely eliminated East Indian immigration because there were no direct steamship links between Indian and Canadian ports.

During the third period immigration was severely reduced at first by World War I and the adjustments of the postwar years. In 1923, the number of immigrants entering Canada began to increase again. Most of the immigrants of the 1920s settled in the industrial and commercial centres of Ontario and Quebec or in the booming resource-based towns of the northern parts of the same provinces. This was a shift from the agriculturally oriented immigration of the second phase. During the 1920s, Canada established a list of "preferred" and "non-preferred" countries. Restrictions against Orientals were continued, with the passage of legislation (1923) virtually excluding all Chinese and a revision (1925) of the "gentlemen's agreement" with Japan further limiting Japanese immigration to an annual quota of 150.

Immigration came to an abrupt halt as a result of the Depression. It is estimated that emigration exceeded immigration by 100 000 during the 1930s. Deportation figures rose during those years as action was taken against immigrants who had become "public charges."

The fourth period has been longer than any other period and has been characterized by a more diverse immigrant population in terms of education, occupation, and ethnic origin. Between 1946 and 1975, 4 249 309 immigrants entered Canada. The total number of immigrants entering Canada during each of 1976 and 1977 was under 200 000 a year.

Immigration policy in the post-World War II period has moved from an ethnically selective basis to an open policy based on predetermined criteria. By 1950, three categories of immigrants were classified as desirable and eligible for admission to Canada. The most favored group included British subjects from the United Kingdom, New Zealand, Australia, and citizens of the United States, Eire, and France.[22] The second eligible group included relatives of legal residents or Canadian citizens. Lastly, other people could only be eligible if they were "citizens of 'non-Asiatic countries' who were 'agriculturists,' miners, or lumbermen entering Canada with 'assured employment.'"[23] The only Orientals to be admitted were unmarried children under 18 and wives of Canadian citizens.

The Immigration Act of 1952 gave the Minister of Citizenship and Immigration the power to limit or prevent the entry of immigrants for any one of several very broadly defined reasons including nationality, ethnic origin, "peculiar" cultural traits, unsuitability for Canadian conditions, and inability to assimilate. Subsequent regulations established different categories of immigrants, ranging from most desirable—hence given easiest access—to least desirable—for whom there were quotas. For example, India was limited to 300 immigrants a year, Pakistan to 100, and Ceylon to 50.[24]

Regulations established by the government in 1962 attempted to eliminate the discriminatory features of previous policies while effectively regulating immigrant inflow at a time of slack economic conditions.[25] The regulations were a compromise, establishing the same criteria for all unsponsored immigrants regardless of origin; at the same time, sponsored immigration, while being liberalized to a degree, was still regulated in relation to the traditional preferred-nonpreferred sources.[26] The criteria for unsponsored immigrants were based on education, training, and skills and were designed to assess the immigrants' likelihood of becoming successfully settled in Canada.

In 1967, the government introduced regulations which removed all nationality and ethnic origin bias in selection criteria and established a third category of immigrants— nominated—in addition to the existing categories of sponsored and independent. The basis of these regulations was a series of nine criteria, popularly called the "points system," used to assess applicants. These criteria were: education and training, personal qualities, occupational demand, occupational skill, age, arranged employment, knowledge of English and/or French, relative in Canada, and area of destination.[27]

Independent immigrants had to obtain at least 50 points out of 100 points on the assessment criteria. Such immigrants were expected to be self-supporting on the basis of their qualifications, after some initial help from the Department of Manpower and Immigration. Nominated immigrants were the responsibility of their nominators, relatives who had to guarantee that their nominees would not become a public charge during their first five years in Canada. The point system of assessment was used and points were awarded on the basis of the immigrant's kinship to his sponsor and whether the sponsor was a landed immigrant or a Canadian citizen. Normally an applicant needed 50 points to be accepted as a nominated immigrant; however, selection officers could select or reject an applicant if important factors affecting the applicant's future success had not been considered.[28] Sponsored immigrants, close relatives of their sponsors, were the direct responsibility of their sponsors. The points system was not used.[29]

In 1974, the assessment criteria were revised to make them more responsive to specific needs of the labor market. Assessment officers were instructed to subtract 10 points from the total points of an applicant who did not have prearranged employment for which Canadian residents were not available or who was not entering a designated occupation. Such occupations are ones for which labor is in short supply in Canada.[30]

Changes in immigration policy between 1949 and 1974 plus other factors including economic conditions in Canada and the sending countries have significantly altered immigration patterns. In 1947, 65 per cent of all immigrants came from the United Kingdom, 13 per cent from the United States, 8 per cent from Poland, and 4 per cent from the Netherlands. Only 10 per cent came from other sources, predominantly other continental European countries.[31] In 1975, about 16 per cent of Canada's immigrants came from the United Kingdom and about 9 per cent from the United States. Forty-three per cent came from Asia, Africa, and the Caribbean.[32] Preliminary figures indicated that trends for 1977 were similar to those for 1975.

A major feature of immigration during the post-World War II period has been the admission of well over 300 000 refugees from Europe, Asia, Africa, and South America, but primarily from Europe. The usual practice is to waive some of the admission requirements and procedures, and special immigration offices are often set up overseas to expedite the processing of applications. Between 1947 and 1952, Canada admitted 124 000 European refugees: persons displaced by the war and its attendant political turmoil. Another major group were the nearly 38 000 Hungarians admitted after the 1956 uprising in Hungary. More recently, refugees have been admitted from Czechoslovakia, Uganda, Vietnam, and Chile, among others.

Immigration since World War II has served to accelerate urbanization; the vast majority of the immigrants have located in towns or cities. For example:

> In 1961, nearly 42 per cent of the residents of Toronto and one-third of the residents of the Toronto metropolitan area were not born in Canada. Twenty-nine per cent of the city's residents and 22 per cent of those in the metropolitan area had immigrated between 1946 and 1961.[33]

One interesting fact, not revealed in the discussion of immigration history, is the low rate of French immigration. In 1926, French immigrants constituted 2.1 per cent of all immigrants, and in 1961, the figure had only risen to 3.1 per cent.[34]

Relatively few of the post-World War II immigrants resident in Quebec have been absorbed into the Francophone community.[35] For example, as of the early 1970s, only 25 per cent of the Italian children registered with the Montreal Catholic school system were attending French schools.[36] Bill 101, passed by the Parti Québécois government in 1977, requires immigrant children, with a few exceptions, to enter the French-language schools. It is the government's hope that this legislation will reverse the traditional movement of immigrants to the Anglophone community.

CURRENT IMMIGRATION POLICY

In 1973, the federal government announced a comprehensive study of immigration policy. The aim of this study was not to produce a government policy statement, but to "set out various policy choices and offer documents and studies to stimulate public discussion."[37] As a result of the work done by the Canadian Immigration and Population Study, the Minister of Manpower and Immigration tabled the Green Paper on Immigration and Population in the House of Commons in 1975. This document outlined four possible immigration policies:

1. retain the present system with no formal limits on numbers or sources
2. retain the present points system and gear it to the state of economy
3. establish targets or maximum numbers on a global, regional, and individual country basis
4. establish a target and specify priorities within the different categories of immigrants, largely related to job skills then in demand.[38]

After considerable public debate and parliamentary debate and investigation, a new Immigration Act was passed in 1977. This Act and subsequent regulations announced in 1978, when the Act was proclaimed, provide for an annual quota on immigration and three categories of immigrants. The quota is reassessed annually on the basis of consultations with the provinces and appropriate groups and organizations.[39]

A family class of immigrants has been established which closely resembles the 1967 sponsored category. Other immigrants, corresponding to the 1967 categories of independent and nominated categories, are selected on the basis of a points system. Applicants with relatives in Canada prepared to assist them in resettling will receive bonus points. The Act incorporates the United Nations' definition of "Convention refugees." The point system will not be applied to these refugees; rather they will be selected on the basis of their ability to adapt to life in Canada, bearing in mind the assistance available to them.[40]

ATTITUDES TOWARD IMMIGRATION

An examination of Canadian immigration history would not be complete without an examination of the attitudes toward immigration and specific groups of immigrants which characterized each period. These attitudes can be understood by a consideration of three categories of questions. The first category includes questions relating to attitudes toward specific groups. Which ethnic groups were considered to be desirable immigrants in each period? Which groups were undesirable? If an ethnic group was differentiated according to social class, how was each class regarded? What impact were undesirable immigrants supposed to have on Canada?

A second category of questions focusses on the attitudes of particular groups in Canadian society. How has each of the charter groups viewed immigration and particular immigrant groups during each period? How have they translated or tried to translate their views into immigration policies? How have the non-British, non-French ethnic groups viewed immigration policy and immigrants from other ethnic origins? How have they sought to influence immigration policy? What outlooks have various social classes and interest groups such as labor, business, and agriculture held toward immigration?

The third category of questions relates to changes in attitudes over time. How have attitudes toward immigration and specific groups changed and for what reasons? Have changed attitudes been reflected in changed policies?

REGIONAL AND RURAL-URBAN SETTLEMENT PATTERNS

By examining immigrant settlement patterns, regional and rural-urban differences appear. The rural-urban differences have been mentioned in relation to the four periods of immigration. In addition to those differences, there are significant regional differences. Over 50 per cent of the immigrants in the 1946-72 period settled in Ontario, while the provinces of Quebec, British Columbia, and Alberta received approximately 36 per cent.[41] In western Canada, as revealed by the 1961 census, 26 per cent of British Columbia's population—the highest in the region—was born outside of Canada, as compared with a low of 16 per cent in Saskatchewan. The same figure is 7 per cent for Quebec and even less in the Atlantic Provinces.[42] This regional distribution of immigration has resulted in the Atlantic Provinces and Quebec (outside of Montreal) remaining largely British or French.[43]

THE IMMIGRANT EXPERIENCE

The study of the immigrant experience brings out the human aspect of immigration in contrast to the topics discussed earlier, which stress patterns, statistics, policies, and motivations—all explored in very general terms. The following short section suggests some significant aspects of the immigrant experience.[44]

In the economic sphere immigrants must find employment or establish themselves in a business or on a farm. Sometimes training and experience acquired in another country are not given full recognition. Language barriers may result in immigrants not obtaining employment in their field and/or may hinder success and mobility on the job. Immigrants are particularly vulnerable to unscrupulous employers and businessmen, both within their group and outside of it, who take advantage of their economic insecurity and unfamiliarity with Canadian practices and laws. In addition, immigrants face myriad new experiences relating to housing, medical care, and other professional and business services.

In the social sphere, the immigrant experience is a complex one. For those not speaking one of the official languages, education in Canada is conducted in a "foreign" language. Children may become more proficient in the new language than in the language of their parents. In many cases, the Canadian educational system represents different values and can convey a value system different from that of the immigrant, thus sparking intergenerational conflict.

In addition to education, immigrants can also face other adjustment problems in the social sphere. Elderly immigrants, sponsored by their families in Canada, are often socially isolated and lonely. Women often may experience social isolation especially if demands of home and/or work make it difficult for them to learn the majority language. As a result of contact with either the English- or French-Canadian community, husbands, and/or wives, may adopt new norms and roles, creating family problems by breaking from tradition. Many immigrants, especially in the fourth period (the post-World War II era), come from rural societies but settle in large urban areas, further complicating adjustment problems.

The willingness of the English- and French-Canadian communities to accept immigrants and specific immigrant groups influences a large part of the immigrant experience, especially in the economic and social spheres. A comparison of the experiences of Chinese immigrants during the 1880s or those of South Asians today with the experiences of English or Scottish immigrants reveals the impact of the majority's attitudes and policies.

The difficulties associated with immigrants' initial adjustment to Canada are often ameliorated by well-established group members or organizations, which exist within the group for this purpose. This is particularly true of ethnic groups exhibiting a high degree of institutional completeness.

INTERETHNIC RELATIONS

There is often a tendency in Canada to define interethnic relations in one or more of the three following ways: English Canadian/French Canadian, ethnic minority group/majority societies, and Native Peoples/Euro-Canadians. The concept interethnic relations, as defined here, refers to the relations, both historical and contemporary, among the ethnic groups that make up Canada. In most cases the significant relations, from the point of view of ethnic groups, have not been between one ethnic group and another but between an ethnic group and one or both of the dominant communities. This is the result of the history and structure of Canadian society with its two charter groups and two dominant communities.

A CONTINUUM OF INTERETHNIC RELATIONS

The best way of examining interethnic relations is through the perspective of a continuum developed by G. E. Simpson, a sociologist.[45] The ends of the continuum are represented by complete segregation and total assimilation. In between those two extremes are limited desegregation, substantial pluralism, hypothetical integration, partial assimilation, group assimilation, and individual assimilation.

Complete segregation. An ethnic group that is completely segregated would be residentially, occupationally, socially, and educationally separate from the dominant society. Theoretically, segregation could exist without resulting social stratification, but in a multiethnic society this is highly unlikely. In reality, the majority would hold negative attitudes toward the segregated group and strong prohibitions would exist to limit interaction to minimal contact through established channels and persons.

Limited desegregation. This very broad concept suggests significant segregation and, obviously, unequal opportunities in the larger society for the segregated group. It would be possible for group members to achieve a high socio-economic status, but they would experience barriers not faced by members of the dominant society. Social interaction between members of the minority group and the majority group would exist, but the general pattern would be one of social isolation for the segregated group. Negative stereotypes would frequently be applied to the segregated group.

Substantial pluralism. A society characterized by substantial pluralism would grant most of its members access to the majority of the opportunities, regardless of ethnic background. Such a society would recognize and respect cultural and social differences of different ethnic groups. However, the range of cultural and social differences accorded respect, recognition, and support might be limited.

Hypothetical integration. Equal opportunities would be freely accorded to all members of all ethnic groups in a hypothetically integrated society. In the social and cultural spheres there would be differences based on ethnicity, and these would be given full opportunity to flourish, provided these "are not in conflict with broader values, patterns, and legal norms common to the entire society."[46]

The remaining three possibilities on the continuum involve varying degrees of assimilation which has been defined as the

> process in which persons of diverse ethnic and racial backgrounds come to interact, free of these constraints, in the life of the larger community. . . . Complete assimilation would mean that no separate social structures based on ethnic or racial concepts remained.[47]

Partial assimilation. The first of the three assimilation positions on the continuum refers to ethnic groups which have experienced some assimilation. For example, the group's culture and social patterns may have disappeared and been replaced by those of the dominant society, but group members still strongly identify with their group.

Group assimilation. When this occurs, members of an ethnic group adopt the social and cultural patterns of the larger society; enter the clubs, organizations, and institutions of the larger society; intermarry freely; and experience a change in their identity, shifting from that of their group to that of the larger society.

Individual assimilation. This has the same meaning as group assimilation only its focus is on the individual and subgroups rather than on the whole group.

THE ASSIMILATION PROCESS

Because of the importance of the process of assimilation in the life of ethnic groups, it is important to pause here and further examine the concept. Milton Gordon, one of the foremost students of intergroup relations, has identified seven subprocesses of assimilation. These are outlined in table 3.

Four of the seven types—cultural, structural, marital, and identificational assimilation—are singled out for particular attention here because they shed the most light on the ethnic group's experience. The other three types—attitude receptional, behavior receptional, and civic assimilation—are both a precondition of structural assimilation and the result of structural assimilation. As prejudice and discrimination against an ethnic group

Table 3/The Assimilation Subprocesses

Subprocess	Type or Stage of Assimilation
Change of cultural patterns to those of host society	Cultural or behavioral assimilation
Large-scale entrance into cliques, clubs, and institutions of host society, on primary group level	Structural assimilation
Large-scale intermarriage	Marital assimilation
Development of sense of peoplehood based exclusively on host society	Identificational assimilation
Absence of prejudice	Attitude receptional assimilation
Absence of discrimination	Behavior receptional assimilation
Absence of value and power conflict	Civic assimilation

Note: Adapted from Milton Gordon, *Assimilation in American Life* (New York: Oxford University Press, 1964), pp. 32-33.

diminish, the doors to structural assimilation are opened; at the same time the increased primary group contact decreases prejudice and discrimination.

The Scots are usually said to be assimilated into the English-Canadian community and this certainly is true relative to other groups such as the Portuguese and Italians. An examination of the Scottish experience according to the seven types of assimilation does, in fact, reveal that large-scale assimilation has taken place in all areas except identificational assimilation. A similar analysis of the Indian experience would reveal that large-scale assimilation has not taken place despite some intermarriage and significant cultural assimilation among Indians in southern Canada. Little assimilation has occurred in five of the seven types—structural, identificational, attitude receptional, behavior receptional, and civic assimilation.

There is sometimes a tendency to see assimilation in terms of all-or-nothing categories; the Germans in Canada are assimilated, the Hutterites are not. Obviously, these kinds of distinctions cloud the issue more than they clarify it. Assimilation should be seen as a process, occurring at various rates within and among ethnic groups and varying according to which stages are being considered.

There are six major variables which affect assimilation rates in Canadian society. The rate of behavioral assimilation is closely related to the degree of similarity between the culture of the ethnic group and that of either the English- or French-Canadian community. Racial and religious differences are the most important factors in impeding structural assimilation. The attitudes held by the larger society and the individual ethnic group, one for the other, play an important part in the process. Ethnic groups with the strongest ethnic identity are least likely to assimilate. The length of time that the ethnic group has been resident in Canada usually is significant. The size of the ethnic group and the majority group affects assimilation rates. The degree of dispersion of the ethnic group among the larger society is also of significance. Ethnic groups living in institutionally complete urban or rural communities tend to assimilate less rapidly. The availability of employment opportunities and the level and transferability of the immigrant's skills and education are important as well. As a general rule, rural immigrants assimilate more slowly than urban immigrants.[48]

SOCIAL AND CULTURAL CHANGE

Several references have been made to social and cultural change earlier in this chapter. Change is best studied in relation to assimilation, the process which is the primary cause of change. As an ethnic group is assimilated into one of the dominant communities, change occurs within the group. This doesn't mean that change cannot occur without assimilation being the cause, but in a multiethnic society change is primarily the result of assimilation.

Basically, social and cultural change affects every part of an ethnic group's culture and social patterns, but changes in language, religion, values, norms, attitudes, roles, and skills are certainly the most important. As a whole group or some of its members—for example, adolescents—abandon all or part of its culture in one area they adopt all or part of the English- or French-Canadian culture in that area. Because the degree and rate of assimilation vary, so do the degree and rate of change. The variables which affect the degree and rate of change are the same as those which affect the process of assimilation.

As a result of change, an ethnic group's culture and social patterns are not the same today as they were when the group entered Canada. Similarly, the cultures and social patterns of an ethnic group in Canada become less and less like that in the group's homeland.

As an ethnic group becomes more like the dominant communities, differentiation and alienation occur within the group. Differentiation is the process by which ethnic group members, as a result of assimilation, become less similar, creating intragroup differences.[49]

Examples of this differentiation can be seen in intergenerational and identificational differences.

As members of an ethnic group experience the process of assimilation and hence become increasingly more at home in the dominant society, they become less at home in their group: the process of alienation.[50] This alienation is most traumatic for bicultural individuals, those who have one foot in a dominant community and one in the ethnic group; their identification is changing and is not exclusively with either group. This alienation occurs most frequently among the children of immigrants. Because of the influences by school, mass media, and peers outside their group, they are not completely at home in their parents' culture. Because of their early socialization and the continuing influence of their family, they are not completely at home in the dominant society. The result is a situation of marginality.

So far, this discussion of change has focussed on assimilation as being the primary cause, but one other cause, though less significant, sheds an interesting light on the ethnic experience. An ethnic group may change by reviving aspects of its original culture and social patterns, which have been temporarily lost or allowed to slip from use. For example, a number of Inuit, unhappy with the change and resultant social problems characteristic of northern settlements, have left these settlements and returned to living off the land.

ETHNIC MINORITY GROUPS AND THEIR STATUS

In any society where there is stratification based on ethnicity, there are ethnic minority groups. However, minority status is not necessarily a rigid thing, nor can precise definition be given of which groups are in this position in Canada at any particular time. The status of the Chinese and Japanese in Canada has undergone major changes since the 1920s. This is especially true of the Japanese, in light of their internment during World War II.

A minority group's status affects the group's self-identity resulting in an

awareness of itself as possessors of a depressed status relative to other groups in society.
A minority group usually senses the fact that it does not fully participate in the life of the larger society.[51]

Often, as a result of their status, members of minority groups sometimes develop attitudes and forms of behavior which further set them apart. This only serves to increase the distance between majority and minority groups. Among members of minorities these attitudes create feelings of inferiority and of being more different than they objectively are.

The definition of ethnic minority groups given earlier stresses two fundamental characteristics: minorities are "set apart" and receive "unequal treatment." In addition, there are voluntary ethnic minority groups, such as the Amish and Hutterites, who chose to set themselves apart and avoid participation in the larger society. The Hutterites and Amish have chosen to "opt out" because their religious beliefs, fundamental to their culture, dictate that the Christian life and salvation can only be achieved by isolating themselves from the "godless" larger society. Such minorities—Hutterites, for example—have been considerably harassed and persecuted because they set themselves apart and pursue a different life-style.

Minority groups, in terms of population, are not necessarily the same as ethnic minority groups in terms of status. The British in Quebec, although a minority in terms of population, are overrepresented, in a statistical sense, in the economic elites in Quebec. The Quiet Revolution and language legislation such as Bill 22 and Bill 101 represent, in part, a reaction by the numerical majority to its minority status in the economic life in Quebec.

Minority groups can react to their status by being pluralistic, assimilationist, secessionist, militant, or submissive.[52] The pluralistic minority seeks to preserve and develop its distinctive way of life, but at the same time desires toleration from the majority and greater degrees of political, social, and economic equality. The goals of such a group are

> achieved when it has succeeded in wresting from the dominant group the fullest measure of equality in all things economic and political and the right to be left alone in all things cultural.[53]

Revitalization is often a part of the struggle of a pluralistic minority. It occurs most often when there has been

> severe cultural deprivation and represents an attempt on the part of ethnic leadership to generate or regenerate a firm sense of positive, ethnic self-identification among (previously) apathetic and/or alienated members of ethnic minorities who had for a long time given up hope of self- or ethnic group betterment.[54]

The economic, educational, and cultural developments occurring on many Indian reserves are examples of this revitalization.

The assimilationist minority seeks complete acceptance by the dominant society. This means the minority is willing to be absorbed and lose its ethnic identity. This assimilation can occur only if the majority is willing to absorb the minority group. It is possible for a minority group to be absorbed without losing its ethnic identity provided the majority does not see that distinctive identity as being incompatible with being a member of the majority. In the Canadian context, an assimilationist minority would be opting for membership in either the English- or French-Canadian communities.

A secessionist minority seeks not only cultural and social independence but also political independence from the society in which it is now a member. Secessionists believe that preservation and development of a distinctive culture and true political and economic equality is not possible without political independence. Canadians are painfully aware of the secessionist goals of the Québecois who support the Parti Québécois. These separatists see themselves as possessors of a minority status in Canada and in their homeland—the province of Quebec—and, hence, see secession or separation as desirable.

A militant minority has goals which extend beyond those of pluralism, assimilation, or independence. It seeks domination over others and "is convinced of its own superiority and inspired by the lust for conquest."[55]

Lastly, a minority group may passively submit to the inferior status assigned to it. No attempts are made to alter its position.

Wherever there is an ethnic minority group there is a possibility of culture conflict, especially if the behavior associated with the minority's values is deemed unacceptable according to the values of the majority group. Such conflicts have occurred over issues such as Hutterite pacifism, Mormon polygamy, and the rejection of compulsory school attendance by some Mennonites. This is when ethnocentrism is in clearest evidence. Prejudice, racism, and discrimination serve to intensify cultural conflicts.

ETHNOCENTRISM, STEREOTYPES, RACISM, PREJUDICE, AND DISCRIMINATION

The previous section examined how ethnic minority groups react to their status as defined by the dominant society. This section examines the dominant society's attitudes and behavior toward the minority group.

Ethnocentrism is the tendency to view and evaluate other people and cultures from the perspective of one's own culture instead of viewing another culture from its own perspective.[56] Children of a particular ethnic group who do not voluntarily answer questions in class are sometimes judged, from the English-Canadian point of view, as being lazy. However, in their own culture they have been taught that such behavior is unacceptable because it indicates a desire to show oneself as being superior. Ethnocentric individuals see their own culture as being the most advanced, refined, or civilized and therefore see other cultures as inferior: the greater the degree of difference, the greater the degree of inferiority.

Ethnic stereotypes are "over-simplified, standardized, and in some respects exaggerated and distorted images . . . applying to an entire ethnic category or group."[57] Stereotypes ignore intragroup differences and label all group members as having the same characteristics. In addition, stereotypes tend to emphasize differences that separate ethnic groups rather than emphasizing similarities. The great range of variation likely existing within the group is not recognized.

The term *racism*, as used in the mass media today, refers to an extreme form of racial prejudice. Social scientists give the term a more precise meaning. Racists associate social and cultural characteristics with racial characteristics; as a result, they believe that it is possible to make qualitative judgments about "races," as they define them, on the basis of these characteristics.[58] Racists see the devotion to duty of ethnic group A as an inherited "racial" quality rather than as a highly prized cultural value. Similarly, they explain the fact that the per capita income of ethnic group B is lower than the national average by calling that "race" lazy.

Racial prejudice refers to negative attitudes or beliefs about an ethnic group because of assumed physical, cultural, and/or social characteristics.[59] *Racial discrimination* refers to behavior directed against an ethnic group based upon the above factors. Its most common form is the denial of opportunities to members of a particular ethnic group.

Research indicates that, in our society, children are born without prejudice and that it is learned at a very early age.[60] If prejudice is not inborn, the question then becomes How do we acquire our prejudices? Three groups of social science theories—economic, psychological, and social norm—will be discussed in this section.[61]

Economic theories revolve around the assumption that it is natural for people to feel negative toward social and economic rivals, especially if the rivalry threatens the dominant group's existing position. It then follows that the threatened group will act to remove the ability of the rival group to be a threat—e.g. by controlling immigration, excluding one or more groups from specific occupations or professions, limiting land holdings, and differentiating hiring practices.

Psychological theories assume that prejudice and discrimination fulfil some psychological need or compensate for some personality defect. The scapegoat theory contends that human beings are unable or unwilling to accept their own weaknesses or failures. The blame is transferred to another group, in this case an ethnic group, which is made the culprit. Immigrants, who are regarded as undercutting Canadian wage rates, are blamed for unemployment among native-born Canadians.

The second psychological theory is that of frustration–aggression. Everyone faces inhibitions and restraints upon their desires, which leads to frustration. Being frustrated leads to an aggressive tendency, a desire to lash out at "some legitimate object toward which . . . aggressiveness and hostility may be directed."[62] An ethnic minority group can serve as that object and in a prejudiced society the individual has a socially acceptable channel for his frustrations.

A body of theory and research has developed around the hypothesis that prejudice is one component of a personality structure "characterized by a rigidity of outlook, suggestibility, gullibility, dislike for ambiguity, anti-scientific and pseudo-scientific attitudes, and unrealistic ideas as to how to achieve their goals."[63] If prejudice is a basic component of a particular personality type, then an understanding of prejudice lies in a study of the origins of that personality type.

The *social norm theory* states that antipathy toward out-group members is a normal and natural part of group living. This theory raises the question:

> Is there any self-conscious people on earth that does not consider itself superior to its neighbors, or at least prefer its own character and ways to those of other people? . . .

> From time immemorial it has been inherent in the very nature of human group identification that the members of any particular group should feel more warmly attracted to other members of their own group than to outsiders.[64]

Identification with one's own group is a part of living as a social group, and this identification leads the individual to think highly of that group. Members of the group share more similarities with each other than they do with members of other groups. Many racial, social, and cultural differences are easily identifiable and make it easy to distinguish between groups. It is possible to hypothesize that the greater the degree of heterogeneity in society, the greater the possibility of widespread intergroup antipathies.

Although this section has explored prejudice and discrimination from the perspective of the dominant group's attitudes and behavior toward minorities, it must be remembered that minorities can be equally prejudiced and equally discriminatory. Minority groups, though, do not possess sufficient power in any of the larger society's institutions to effectively discriminate against anyone. However, they can discriminate within their sub-societies, specifically, in the area of primary relationships.

THE IMPACT OF ETHNIC DIVERSITY

Despite the difficulties experienced by Canadians in defining their national character, there is widespread popular consensus that Canada is an ethnic mosaic. This social image, as popularly defined, implies that ethnic groups have been able to preserve and develop their culture while integrating fully into the economic, political, cultural, and social spheres of Canadian life, if they so wish. This section explores, from a social science perspective, the validity of this image, and looks at the larger question of the impact of ethnic diversity on Canadian life.

ETHNIC MOSAIC

The following two questions are central to determining if Canada is, in fact, an ethnic mosaic: (1) Are all ethnic groups proportionately represented in the various occupational levels and in the economic, political, social, and cultural elites? (2) Do ethnic groups preserve and evolve distinctive cultural patterns?

The sociological research of John Porter is relevant to question (1). He uses the terms "over-representation" and "under-representation" in reporting on ethnic group-occupation relationships.[65] Over-representation exists when an ethnic group holds a greater proportion of the positions in a particular occupational category than the proportion that group represents of the total labor force. Under-representation means that the ethnic group holds less than its share of the positions in an occupational category. In 1961, the British were over-represented in the professional and financial (+2.0) and clerical (+1.3) categories, and the Jews were over-represented in the professional and financial category (+7.4). All other European ethnic groups were under-represented in these two categories. The Italians (+11.5), French (+2.8), Indians and Inuit (+34.7), and "Other European" (+1.8) were over-represented in the primary and unskilled category. The British (-2.3), Germans (-2.1), Jews (-8.9), Dutch (-2.0), and Scandinavians (-.2) were all under-represented in the same category.[66] Elsewhere in the same study Porter concluded that "As far as ethnic background is concerned, it is clear that preference for recruitment to the economic elite is for English-speaking people of British origin."[67]

On the basis of Porter's study, it does not appear that large-scale integration has taken place in Canada. However, several cautions must be applied to these findings. First of all, the data used in this study, based on the 1961 census, are now somewhat out-of-date (though it is unlikely that the basic patterns have changed greatly in the intervening years). Secondly, the data do not distinguish between those of a particular ethnic origin who have been assimilated into one of the dominant communities and those who are members of the ethnic group of their origin. Lastly, the data do not differentiate between Canadian- and foreign-born members of an ethnic group. Variables such as language and educational opportunities in the home country may account for some of the differences in occupational representation among immigrants.

Another study, relevant to this discussion, investigated ethnic representation in the following elites: corporate, labor, political, civil service, communications, and academic.[68] This study, carried out in Toronto, found that in none of the six spheres had the proportion of non-Anglo-Saxons in the elites reached the proportion of non-Anglo-Saxons in the community's population as a whole.[69] When the structure of the elites was compared with that of twenty years previous, non-Anglo-Saxon representation had increased considerably. The rate of increase of entrance into the elites varies considerably among ethnic groups, Jews having been most successful to date.

On the basis of the two studies discussed above, Canada is not an ethnic mosaic when the concept of integration is used as a measuring stick. The title of Porter's study *The Vertical Mosaic* more aptly describes Canadian society than the popular ethnic mosaic image.

Question (2) relates to cultural preservation and development as part of an ethnic mosaic. This area is much more difficult to investigate empirically in contrast to integration. Such an investigation would involve comparing selected aspects of the culture and social patterns of second- and third-generation Canadians with those of first-generation Canadians of the same origin, and one or both of the two dominant communities. The complexities of making comparisons across time and cultures are legion and, to date, this kind of research has not been done.

For this reason it is only possible to discuss the issue of cultural preservation and development in the most general terms. With the exception of isolated groups such as the Hutterites, Amish, Old Order Mennonites, and some groups of Indians and Inuit, the pattern among ethnic groups has been the disappearance, over time and at varying rates, of ethnic cultures. Largely as the result of industrialization, urbanization, Americanization, and the influence of the mass media, the cultural content of all ethnic groups is becoming similar. As one sociologist has said, the difference between a Polish professional today and his peasant grandfather is greater than that between a Polish professional and a Greek professional today.[70] This growing similarity among ethnic cultures in Canada today does not preclude identifying with the ethnic group of one's origin. The cultural content of ethnic groups is becoming more similar, but the identification remains.[71]

IMPACT OF ETHNIC DIVERSITY

The following questions provide a focus for the study of the impact of ethnic diversity on Canada's society and culture.

What role have non-British, non-French Canadians played in the development of Canada's economy, political system, social structure and non-material culture, and artistic and folk culture?

How have the English- and French-Canadian communities been affected, since 1867, by the growth of ethnic diversity?

What impact will increasing ethnic diversity have on Canada's development in the future?

Though little information is available to answer such questions, that does not negate their importance.

This theme is often thought of in terms of an ethnic group's contributions to Canadian society. Many ethnic groups, in studies of their own history in Canada, tend to stress the contributions of great people in the arts, agriculture, politics, science, and business. A more general approach is used here because it reveals more about the totality of the ethnic experience and facilitates comparisons.

In addition to the constraint resulting from lack of relevant data, there are three other cautions to consider here. First, it is impossible to generalize about the impact of ethnic diversity without considering differences among ethnic groups. Second, regional differences in the ethnic composition of the population make it impossible to generalize about all of Canada. Third, it is important to recognize that ethnic groups vary in degree of differentiation and that such differentiation makes the impact of ethnic diversity an even more complex issue.

One historian, H. D. Palmer, has explored the impact of ethnic diversity on Alberta, particularly southern Alberta.[72] Although the findings of his study are relevant only to that region, they do provide a framework for studying this topic.

Economy. In this sphere, the impact of ethnic diversity can be examined from the perspective of economic development in areas such as transportation, agriculture, construction, natural resources, manufacturing, and service industries. Has economic development been furthered in one or more of these areas by members of one or more ethnic groups? What has been the nature of their contribution—unskilled labor, technical skills, capital, entrepreneurship, or market? In addition, have ethnic group members been upwardly mobile?

Political system. In this sphere, consideration revolves around the impact of ethnic diversity on politics. Have certain groups or subgroups tended to support certain parties or adopt particular stances on political issues? The political concerns of ethnic groups and the response these groups received from politicians and political parties are of equal importance. Political participation by ethnic group members may be assessed in terms of involvement in political parties, campaigning activities, candidacies for various parties and levels of government, and representation in various levels of government.

Social structure and non-material culture. Turning next to either or both English- or French-Canadian social structure and non-material culture, the most important point of departure would be an examination of the impact of diversity on attitudes, values, norms, roles, and religious beliefs. Has diversity encouraged conservative or liberal values, norms, and roles? Has diversity created social conflict? Has greater social mobility been the outcome of a progressively more pluralistic society? Has the speed and nature of social change been influenced by ethnic diversity?

Artistic and folk culture. Looking at Canadian culture in the artistic and folk sense, have the themes expressed in literature, television, opera, and drama; folk, rock, and classical music; and film reflected the ethnic experience or diversity? When themes reflect ethnicity what are the opinions, attitudes, and values expressed in these? Has the development of any one of the above art forms been encouraged by members of any one ethnic group? Some immigrants have become involved in certain cultural pursuits and influenced the direction of their development by infusing new styles and modes of expression from the home country. Many ethnic groups sponsor activities related to aspects of their folk culture. Have Canadians of other heritages become involved in these, either as observers or participants, to a significant degree?

WHAT IS CANADA TO BECOME?

In October 1971, Prime Minister Trudeau announced in the House of Commons that the federal government was adopting a policy of "multiculturalism within a bilingual framework." Canada would retain its two official languages, but instead of one or more official cultures there would be no official culture. Under this policy the government would

> support and encourage the various cultures and ethnic groups that give structure and vitality to our society. They will be encouraged to share their cultural expression and values with other Canadians and so contribute to a richer life for us all.[73]

The "bilingual framework" had been established by the Official Languages Act of 1969 which had made English and French official languages in areas of federal jurisdiction, established bilingual districts, and created the position of Commissioner of Official Languages to act as a "watchdog," ensuring that the spirit of the Act is carried out.

The policy of multiculturalism, as announced in 1971, had four objectives:

> First, the Government of Canada will support all of Canada's cultures and will seek to assist, resources permitting, the development of those cultural groups which have demonstrated a desire and effort to continue to develop, a capacity to grow and contribute to Canada, as well as a clear need for assistance.
>
> Second, the government will assist members of all cultural groups to overcome cultural barriers to full participation in Canadian society.
>
> Third, the government will promote creative encounters and interchange among all Canadian cultural groups in the interest of national unity.
>
> Fourth, the government will continue to assist immigrants to acquire at least one of Canada's official languages in order to become full participants in Canadian society.[74]

This policy of multiculturalism had its origins in the Royal Commission on Bilingualism and Biculturalism. The Commission in Book IV of its Report addressed itself to the question of "the contribution made by the other ethnic groups to the cultural enrichment of Canada."[75] The commissioners found a "collective will to exist"[76] among ethnic groups and stressed the enrichment Canada gains from its ethnic diversity. They made sixteen recommendations emphasizing the recognition of the non-British non-French ethnic fact in Canada. The federal government's acceptance of the Commission's recommendations was encouraged by a growing appreciation of ethnic diversity among the Canadian public and forceful arguments from ethnic leaders at the Commission's hearings and elsewhere.

Six programs to implement the policy's objectives were announced along with the policy statement. These programs, administered by the Multiculturalism Directorate of the Department of the Secretary of State, were:

- grants to ethnic groups
- research into the relationship between language and culture
- the writing of ethnic histories
- encouragement of scholarly research
- teaching of the official languages
- specific programs within federal cultural agencies, such as the National Film Board.

Since 1971, four provinces—Ontario, Manitoba, Saskatchewan, and Alberta—have given official recognition and support, in varying ways, to the cultural diversity characteristic of each province.

FOUR MODELS

Although the federal government has adopted a policy of multiculturalism, there should be an ongoing examination of the policy to determine if it is the most appropriate one for Canada. This section presents four models which are useful in understanding Canadian society past, present, and future: the melting pot, Anglo-conformity, Anglo- and Franco-conformity, and multiculturalism or cultural pluralism. These models represent ideal types rather than attempts at portraying empirical realities. No one of these models alone accurately describes Canadian society past or present because models are, by definition, intellectual tools used to facilitate understanding.[77]

The melting pot. This model implies that all ethnic groups within a society will blend together to form a "new man." It "leaves no room for the overt persistence of the ancestral culture, social institutions or ethnic identity of either (any) group in contact."[78]

The melting pot is a two-way transaction among ethnic groups, each group making a contribution to the new culture and each group changing significantly. There is no room for one or more dominant groups. In such a society there would be no barriers to full integration of all members, if they are prepared to "melt" into the new society.

Anglo-conformity. In this model, all people who are not of British heritage would be assimilated into the British culture. Assimilation would be unidirectional. There would be only one official language—English—and non-British cultures would have to be relegated to history. There is a notion of the superiority of the British culture implicit in such a model. Before integration could occur there would have to be full behavioral assimilation. Ethnic groups entering such a society would be assigned a lower status upon arrival, and they could only move from it by being assimilated.

Anglo- and Franco-conformity. This model is somewhat similar to Anglo-conformity except that there are two cultures and languages rather than one. All members of the non-charter groups would be expected to assimilate into one of the cultures. The same type of barrier to integration would exist as in the case of Anglo-conformity.

Multiculturalism or cultural pluralism. This model gives each ethnic group the opportunity to develop and preserve its culture. There would have to be some limits on the degree of diversity in order that the society would function as a whole.

> Any society, if it is to survive, must have a considerable agreement among its members as to basic ideals, goals, values, mores, folkways, and beliefs. An aggregation of individuals, or of groups, each speaking its own language, worshiping its own gods, practicing its own sex mores, following its own peculiar customs with respect to food, dress, recreation, and government would not be a society at all.[79]

No one has attempted to draw the fine line between the behavioral assimilation necessary for a functioning society and the diversity characteristic of a pluralistic society. Without some behavioral assimilation, full integration would not be possible. There would be no barriers to integration, beyond the behavioral assimilation mentioned above.

In the area of language policy multilingualism would accompany multiculturalism. Multilingualism could exist in one of two forms: there could be one or more working languages and official encouragement for other languages; or there could be no working language—all languages would be used and encouraged. The latter form of multilingualism would only be feasible in societies with a limited number of ethnic groups.

In the area of primary relationships ethnic group members would tend to associate with others of their group, thus creating voluntary segregation. There would be no prejudice, discrimination, or high levels of ethnocentrism associated with this segregation. Cultural preservation and development can only occur if there is voluntary segregation.

Throughout this chapter concepts related to the nature and degree of the ethnic diversity which is an integral and significant part of Canadian society have been explored. It is an inescapable fact that this diversity will continue to be an important feature of our society in the years ahead. Canadians must accept the responsibility of evaluating current social and cultural policies relevant to this diversity, examining the various options before them, and thinking of the goals they seek for their society and culture. The concepts discussed in this chapter should guide such an inquiry.

Notes

1. Frank G. Vallee, "Multi-ethnic Societies: The Issues of Identity and Inequality," in *Issues in Canadian Society: An Introduction to Sociology*, ed. D. Forcece and S. Richer (Scarborough: Prentice-Hall, 1975), p. 167.

2. Ibid., p. 165.

3. Wsevolod W. Isajiw, "Olga in Wonderland, Ethnicity in Technological Society," *Canadian Ethnic Studies*, vol. 9, no. 1, 1977, pp. 77-78.

4. Vallee, "Multi-ethnic Societies," p. 167.

5. George A. Theodorson and Achilles G. Theodorson, *A Modern Dictionary of Sociology,* quoted in Vallee, "Multi-ethnic Societies," p. 164.

6. John Porter, *The Vertical Mosaic: An Analysis of Social Class and Power in Canada* (Toronto: University of Toronto Press, 1965), p. 60.

7. Jean Leonard Elliott, "Minority Groups: A Canadian Perspective," in *Minority Canadians 2: Immigrant Groups* (Scarborough: Prentice-Hall, 1971), p. 2.

8. Louis Wirth, "The Problem of Minority Groups," in *Minority Responses: Comparative Views of Reactions to Subordination,* ed. Minako Kurokawa (New York: Random House, 1970), pp. 34–35.

9. Milton Gordon, *Assimilation in American Life: The Role of Race, Religion, and National Origins* (New York: Oxford University Press, 1964), pp. 32-33.

10. Ibid., p. 33.

11. Tamotsu Shibutani and Kian M. Kwan, *Ethnic Stratification: A Comparative Approach* (New York: Macmillan, 1965), pp. 57-58.

12. Alphonsus P. Campbell, "The Heritage of the Highland Scots in Prince Edward Island," *Revue de l'Université d'Ottawa,* vol. 44, no. 1, 1974, p. 53.

13. Canada, Royal Commission on Bilingualism and Biculturalism, *Report of the Royal Commission on Bilingualism and Biculturalism: Book IV, The Cultural Contribution of the Other Ethnic Groups* (Ottawa, Information Canada, 1970), p. 93.

14. Milton M. Gordon, "Assimilation in America: Theory and Reality," in *Majority and Minority: The Dynamics of Racial and Ethnic Relations,* ed. Norman R. Yetman and C. Hoy Steele (Boston: Allyn and Bacon, 1971), p. 279.

15. Raymond Breton, "Institutional Completeness of Ethnic Communities and Personal Relations of Immigrants," in *Canada: A Sociological Profile,* ed. W. E. Mann (Toronto: Copp Clark, 1968), p. 191.

16. Ibid., pp. 193-94.

17. Canada, RCBB, *The Cultural Contribution,* p. 111.

18. Ibid., p. 107.

19. Unless otherwise noted, the discussion of the four periods of immigration is based on Canada, RCBB, *The Cultural Contribution,* pp. 17-30.

20. Mabel F. Timlin, "Canada's Immigration Policy, 1890-1910," *Canadian Journal of Economics and Political Science,* vol. 24, no. 4, 1960, p. 517.

21. Canada, RCBB, *The Cultural Contribution,* pp. 22-23.

22. George Rawlyk, "Canada's Immigration Policy, 1945-1962," *Dalhousie Review,* vol. 42, no.3, 1962, p. 290.

23. Ibid., p. 291.

24. Ibid., p. 292.

25. Canada, Department of Manpower and Immigration, Canadian Immigration and Population Study, *The Immigration Program* (Ottawa: Information Canada, 1974), p. 28.

26. Ibid.

27. Ibid., p. 59.

28. Ibid., p. 60.

29. Ibid., pp. 52-54.

30. Ibid., p. 60.

31. Rawlyk, "Canada's Immigration Policy," p. 291.

32. Dean Wood and Robert Remnant, *The People We Are: Canada's Multicultural Society* (Agincourt, Ont.: Gage, forthcoming), chapter 3.

33. Canada, RCBB, *The Cultural Contribution,* p. 29.

34. Warren E. Kalbach and Wayne W. McVey, *The Demographic Bases of Canadian Society* (Toronto: McGraw-Hill, 1971), p. 38.

35. Anthony E. Richmond, "Immigration and Pluralism in Canada," *International Migration Review,* vol. 4, no. 1, 1969, p. 12.

36. Kenneth McRoberts and Dale Posgate, *Quebec: Social Change and Political Crisis* (Toronto: McClelland and Stewart, 1976), p. 137.

37. R. M. Tait, "The Canadian Immigration and Population Study," *Alternatives,* vol. 3, no. 3, 1974, p. 18.

38. Canada, Department of Manpower and Immigration, Information Service, George Bonavia, *Focus on Canadian Immigration* (Ottawa, 1977), pp. 12-14.

39. "Focus on Immigration," *Ethnic Kaleidoscope Canada,* December 1977, p. 22.

40. Ibid., pp. 20-21.

41. Edith Ferguson, *Immigrants in Canada* (Toronto: Guidance Centre, Faculty of Education, University of Toronto, 1974), p. 14.

42. Canada, RCBB, *The Cultural Contribution,* p. 31.

43. Ibid.

44. Ferguson, *Immigrants in Canada,* pp. 18-27.

45. *International Encyclopedia of the Social Sciences,* vol. 1, s.v. "Assimilation," by George Eaton Simpson, p. 438.

46. Milton M. Gordon, "Social Structure and Goals in Group Relations," in *Freedom and Control in Modern Society,* ed. Morroe Berger, Theodore Abel, and Charles H. Page (New York: D. Van Nostrand, 1954), p. 153.

47. *International Encyclopedia of the Social Sciences,* vol. 1, p. 438.

48. Howard Palmer, *Land of the Second Chance: A History of Ethnic Groups in Southern Alberta* (Lethbridge: Lethbridge Herald, 1972), p. 255.

49. Frank G. Vallee, M. Schwarz, and F. Darknell, "Ethnic Assimilation and Differentiation in Canada," in *Canadian Society: Sociological Perspectives,* 3d ed., ed. R. R. Blishen et al. (Toronto: Macmillan, 1968), p. 594.

50. M. L. Kovacs and A. J. Cropley, "Assimilation and Alienation in Ethnic Groups," *Canadian Ethnic Studies,* vol. 4, nos. 1-2, 1972, p. 16.

51. Elliott, *Minority Canadians 2,* p.2.

52. Wirth, "The Problem of Minority Groups," pp. 36-41 and David Hughes and Evelyn Kallen, *The Anatomy of Racism: Canadian Dimensions* (Montreal: Harvest House, 1974), p. 203.

53. Wirth, "The Problem of Minority Groups," p. 37.

54. Hughes and Kallen, *The Anatomy of Racism,* p. 203.

55. Wirth, "The Problem of Minority Groups," p. 41.

56. Hughes and Kallen, *The Anatomy of Racism,* p. 89.

57. Ibid., p. 91.

58. Pierre L. van den Berghe, *Race and Racism: A Comparative Perspective* (New York: John Wiley and Sons, 1976), p. 11.

59. Hughes and Kallen, *The Anatomy of Racism,* p. 105.

60. Brewton Berry, *Race and Ethnic Relations,* 3d ed. (Boston: Houghton Mifflin Co., 1965), p. 305.

61. Ibid., pp. 304-315.

62. Ibid., p. 310.

63. Ibid., p. 311.

64. H. P. Fairchild, *Race and Nationality,* quoted in Berry, *Race and Ethnic Relations,* p. 313.

65. Porter, *The Vertical Mosaic,* p.76.

66. Ibid., p. 87.

67. Ibid., p. 287.

68. Merrijoy Kelner, "Ethnic Penetration into Toronto's Elite Structure," in *Social Space: Canadian*

Perspectives, ed. D. I. Davies and Kathleen Herman (Toronto: New Press, 1971), p. 188.

69. Ibid., p. 188.

70. Jean Burnet, Address to The Social Sciences in Canada Symposium, University of Calgary, 4 February 1977.

71. Ibid.

72. Palmer, *Land of the Second Chance,* pp. 220-60.

73. Prime Minister Pierre Elliott Trudeau, Statement to the House of Commons, 8 October 1971.

74. Ibid.

75. Canada, RCBB, *The Cultural Contribution,* p. 3.

76. Trudeau, Statement to the House of Commons.

77. Hughes and Kallen, *The Anatomy of Racism,* p. 183.

78. Ibid., p. 185.

79. Berry, *Race and Ethnic Relations,* p. 224.

CHAPTER 3

Five Units of Curriculum and Instruction in Ethnic Studies

INTRODUCTION

This chapter presents five units of curriculum and instruction in ethnic studies for use in junior and senior high school Canada studies, social studies, history, and sociology programs. The units are flexible in design and lend themselves to whatever the needs and interests of a teacher may be.

The chapter is organized into five major units, parallelling the themes explored in chapter 2. Three of the five units are subdivided into topics. Each unit or topic contains suggestions regarding objectives, teaching strategies, and instructional materials. The instructional materials are referred to by number, corresponding to the numbered items in the Selected Bibliography, chapter 4.

Although at first glance the units may appear to be highly structured and prescriptive, this is not the case. The references to objectives, teaching strategies, and instructional materials are designed to aid the process of instructional planning, not replace it. In essence, the framework is provided and teachers can refine it to suit their instructional goals, educational philosophy, and students' needs.

In most units and topics a large number of references is suggested. This extensive listing is provided so that teachers can make selections according to availability, reading level, and interest level.

Not all units and topics need necessarily be studied in every classroom. Factors such as program specifications, interest, time, and resources will influence the number and nature of the topics selected. Although these units are designed to be a self-contained entity in a Canada studies program, selected units and topics can find ready application in sociology and Canadian history and society courses. For example, a study of Unit 2—Immigration— would be of significance in a history course and topics from Unit 3 could be relevant to a study of minority groups and prejudice and discrimination in a sociology course.

Throughout this chapter there are continual references to guiding questions. Such questions are used to give direction to students' inquiry and focus their attention on the data central to the study. They differ from other forms of questions in that they are derived from a conceptual background and are focussed on a topic rather than on the instructional materials. Guiding questions are usually general in nature and encourage skill-related learning rather than the search for the right page, paragraph, and sentence that answers a specific rote-learning question. Examples of guiding questions are provided on p. 46.

These questions can be developed by the teacher after a reading of the relevant section in chapter 2 and/or teacher-student interaction. By asking students a question such as "What do we need to know in order to understand the causes of prejudice and discrimination in Canada?" teachers will be able to elicit guiding questions as well as train students in an important phase of inquiry.

Jack R. Fraenkel's *Helping Students Think and Value: Strategies for Teaching the Social Studies* (Englewood Cliffs, N.J.: Prentice-Hall, 1973) is a useful resource book for the teaching strategies mentioned in this chapter.

UNIT 1/WHAT IS AN ETHNIC GROUP?

Topic A

Theme: Introduction and community study

Teacher Reference: pp. 7, 8, 9

OBJECTIVES
Students will be able to
1. make statements about ethnic diversity in Canada based on viewing films
2. express their opinions in response to questions about ethnic diversity
3. identify how information in the films contradicts, supports, or raises questions about their perceptions of ethnic groups
4. define ethnic group
5. describe their family history, highlighting their ethnic heritages
6. identify symbols of ethnic diversity in their community

TEACHING STRATEGIES
Objective 1. Perhaps the best way to introduce students to ethnic studies is through the use of film; its immediacy and drama make it intrinsically motivating. In addition, the use of film provides students with a variety of perspectives and a considerable body of information in a short time. For these reasons, the first three objectives of Topic A will be based on a so-called ethnic film festival utilizing several of the National Film Board films listed below.

Films: 218, 303, 335, 381, 384, 428, 496, 497, 540, 559, 585, 610, 635, 652, 710, 745.

After each film or series of films, students can be asked to discuss the following questions:
— What is a Canadian?
— Do all Canadians live in the same way?
— Do all Canadians have the same goals?
— What different life styles and goals are portrayed in the films?
— Why are there differences?
— Is there prejudice and discrimination in Canada?
— Have all Canadians had equal opportunities?
— How do the people portrayed in the films feel about their heritages?
— How do these films relate to a study of Canada?

Objective 2. Encourage students to discuss questions such as:
— Why, in your opinion, do some Canadians maintain a strong attachment to their distinctive way of life and their heritage?

- Are the ways of life portrayed in the films good or bad for Canada?
- Should Canadians preserve and develop their unique cultures?
- How would you feel if you had had the same experiences as some of the people in the films?
- Why, in your opinion, have some Canadians been victims of prejudice and discrimination?
- What should be done about prejudice and discrimination?

Objective 3. The approach for this objective is the same as for 1 and 2. The discussion questions are:
- What were your impressions of each group before you saw the films?
- Does the information in the film support, contradict, or raise questions about your previous impressions?
- What questions and issues do these films suggest?

Objective 4. Tell students that each film portrayed a different ethnic group. Have students suggest characteristics which these groups have in common. Discuss each characteristic and determine its validity. Develop a comprehensive and concise definition in this manner.

If films were not used to introduce this topic, then several readings should be used to accomplish objectives 1 to 3 in much the same manner. Teachers should resist defining ethnic group for students, because the inductive approach encompasses important learning opportunities; in addition, students need an initial information base, either through films or readings. This background provides a common departure point and gives teachers an opportunity to assess the knowledge and attitudes students bring to this study.

Objective 5. One way students can understand the personal relevance of ethnic studies is by preparing a family tree and a family history. The family tree should contain the name of each ancestor, place of birth, and ethnic origin. Teachers should guide students, by means of a class discussion, in the development of a set of key questions to use when investigating their family histories. Some sample questions are:
- Why did your parents or ancestors decide to immigrate to Canada?
- What did they think of Canada when they first arrived?
- Do they celebrate the holidays and festivals of their ethnic group?
- Do they still speak their language?

Bearing in mind the cautions stated below, a class can develop, after completing this assignment, a summary of the places of birth and ethnic origins represented in the class. Similarly, topics such as the immigrant experience and cultural retention can be discussed.

A few cautions about family trees and histories are in order. Teachers should know their class well before setting this task because it might create embarrassment for some children. Will some parents or grandparents regard such questions as an invasion of privacy and refuse to cooperate? Will children of single-parent families be embarrassed by having only "half" a family to report on? Is there any danger that immigrant children and families will think this task singles them out because they are "different"? Sensitivity on the teacher's part can go a long way toward eliminating most of the above difficulties. This task could be paired with several other different types of assignments and students could then be given a choice.

If teachers foresee no major problems in this area and wish to make this assignment into a major project, a little book *Understanding You and Them* (chap. 4/153) provides an excellent series of questions and ideas on preparing family histories stressing the ethnic dimension.

Objective 6. Students' awareness of ethnic diversity in their own town or city can be heightened in various ways: a class field trip, small group surveys, a panel discussion, interviews, and telephone directory surveys.

Class field trip. This could include visits to ethnic residential and business districts, cultural centres, museums with ethnic displays, social service agencies assisting immigrants, and ethnic organizations.

Small group survey. This type of community study involves assigning an area of the town or city to several students and having them do a walking tour of the area, identifying the symbols of ethnic diversity found there. They could look for ethnic churches, businesses, theatres, restaurants, halls, cultural activities, and neighborhoods. Their report could take the form of essay, oral presentation, or photo essay.

Panel discussion. Representatives from ethnic organizations, government agencies, and social service agencies could discuss topics related to the immigrant experience, cultural retention, the concerns and goals of ethnic organizations, and prejudice and discrimination. Each panelist could make a short presentation and a question period could follow.

Interviews. Students could interview people in their community. This would work well in small communities where students would know many people and their backgrounds. Teachers should assist students in selecting interviewees so that they interview both immigrants and Canadian-born people maintaining an affiliation with their ethnic group.

Telephone directory survey. Students can survey the yellow pages of the telephone directory, using headings such as restaurants, churches, clubs, halls, associations and societies, social service organizations, and specific ethnic headings such as Chinese and Indian. This last approach is perhaps the least satisfactory of the five but does at least alert students to ethnic diversity in their community.

In each of the above community studies there should be an in-class orientation considering questions such as: What are we studying? What information do we want to obtain? How are we going to obtain this information? After the community study, follow-up activities should be pursued. Did we obtain the information we sought? If not, why? How can we compile our findings? What conclusions can we draw from our information about ethnic diversity in our town or city?

Topic B

Key Concepts: Ethnic origin, ethnic identity, race, nationality, immigrant, charter group, Anglophone, Francophone, English-Canadian community, French-Canadian community, and ethnic minority group.

Teacher Reference: pp. 7, 8, 9

OBJECTIVES
Students will be able to
1. define ethnic origin and describe Canada's population in terms of ethnic origin
2. define ethnic identity and discuss related questions
3. define race, nationality, immigrant, charter group, Anglophone, Francophone, English-Canadian community, French-Canadian community, and ethnic minority group

TEACHING STRATEGIES
Objective 1. Explain the meaning of ethnic origin. Have students prepare a bar or circle graph, illustrating the ethnic origin of the Canadian population.

References: 13 (p. 71), 25 (chap. 1), or 107 (pp. 206-7)

Objective 2. Explain the meaning of ethnic identification. Discuss:
— What feelings and attitudes are a part of ethnic identification?
— What indicators can we use to measure identification?
— Why do some people identify with their group more than other people do?
— If people do not identify with their group, will they participate in the group's activities, share their concerns, and associate with group members?
— Similarly, what about people with strong ethnic identification? What is the relationship, as a general rule, between ethnic identification and participation?

Objective 3. These terms can be explained with a lecture based on information in the teacher reference section.

Topic C

Generalization: An ethnic group is characterized by a distinctive culture.

Teacher Reference: pp. 10, 11

OBJECTIVES
Students will be able to
1. describe one or more ethnic cultures, emphasizing the non-material aspects such as values, attitudes, and norms
2. list and compare and contrast the values of the culture(s) under study
3. compare and contrast the values of several groups with their own values
4. list and compare and contrast the norms of the culture(s) under study
5. compare and contrast the norms of several cultures with those common in English-Canadian society
6. explain how the values and norms of a particular group would affect the members' perceptions of various behaviors and issues
7. define ethnic culture
8. analyse a new reading according to objectives 1 and 7

TEACHING STRATEGIES
Objective 1. Through group or independent study and using guiding questions developed by the teacher or through teacher-student interaction, students will develop a knowledge of several ethnic cultures.

References:
Amish—*186*
Chinese—*258*
East Indians—*297*
Greeks—*383*
Hutterites—*25, 389, 392, 398, 399*
Indians—*25, 424, 428, 429, 482, 503, 694*

Jews—*607, 610*
Mennonites—*23, 633, 635, 637, 638*
Québécois—*25, 354*
Scots—*25, 723*
Ukrainians—*25, 748*

Objective 2. Have students list the values (approximately five) which they think are central to each of the cultures studied above. It is usually not possible to identify more than five to seven values on the basis of one reading. The Rokeach Value Survey, reproduced below, might be useful as a starting point. Caution students to try and perceive each of the values from the perspective of its culture; also caution them that the reading might not be typical of the whole group (e.g. Old Order Mennonites). Through class discussion, compare and contrast the values of several ethnic groups.

Rokeach Value Survey
1. A comfortable life (a prosperous life)
2. An exciting life (a stimulating, active life)
3. A sense of accomplishment (lasting contribution)
4. A world of peace (free of war and conflict)
5. A world of beauty (beauty of nature and the arts)
6. Equality (brotherhood, equal opportunity for all)
7. Family security (taking care of loved ones)
8. Freedom (independence, free choice)
9. Happiness (contentedness)
10. Inner harmony (freedom from inner conflict)
11. Mature love (sexual and spiritual intimacy)
12. National security (protection from attack)
13. Pleasure (an enjoyable, leisurely life)
14. Salvation (saved, eternal life)
15. Self-respect (self-esteem)
16. Social recognition (respect, admiration)
17. True friendship (close companionship)
18. Wisdom (a mature understanding of life)

Source: Milton Rokeach, "Conceptualizing the Role of Values in Education," in *Developing Value Constructs in Schooling: Inquiry into Process and Product*, ed. James A. Phillips (Ohio Association for Supervision and Curriculum Development, 1972), pp. 7-8.

Objective 3. Have students identify the five most important values in their value systems, again using the Rokeach Value Survey as a starting point. In a paragraph, or through class discussion, students can state the similarities and differences between their own values and those of the ethnic cultures under study. Students should consider the reasons for the similarities and differences they identify.

Objectives 4 and 5. These can be approached in much the same manner as 2 and 3. Identify the norms of each culture (again the readings will present limitations) and have students compare them with their own. As in objective 3, stress the search for reasons for the similarities and differences.

Objective 6. Present students with a list of controversial issues and examples of interpersonal behaviors such as those listed below. Divide the class into groups, each group representing a culture studied for objective 1. How would members of that culture react to each item on the list? Examples:
- welfare recipients who refuse to work
- divorce
- parental discipline of teenagers
- the importance of religion in society
- flooding a large area of a province to provide hydro-electric power
- the importance of romantic love in marriage
- the importance of education
- upward social and economic mobility
- intermarriage
- dating.

Each group could report its conclusions to the class; then the class could discuss the reasons for the similarities and differences that emerged. What impact can the values and norms of a culture have on the perceptions and behavior of group members? Will the degree of impact vary from one individual to another? Why?

Objective 7. Distribute a list of general statements about ethnic groups. Examples:
- Each ethnic group has made a contribution to the Canadian mosaic.
- Each ethnic group has a definition of the good life.
- Ethnic groups which have experienced discrimination occupy a lower socio-economic level today.
- The significance attached to material success varies among ethnic groups.

Have students select those which are attributes of an ethnic culture. Using this exercise as a starting point, formulate, through class discussion, a definition of ethnic culture.

Objective 8. Working independently, students can prepare a written assignment on the culture of a group on the basis of the questions in objective 1 and the definition in objective 7. This assignment could be used in place of a test on this topic.

Topic D

Generalization: An ethnic group is characterized by distinctive social patterns.

Teacher Reference: pp. 11, 12

OBJECTIVES
Students will be able to
1. describe the social patterns of one or more ethnic groups
2. compare and contrast the social patterns of two or more groups
3. define ethnic social patterns
4. analyse a new reading according to objectives 1 and 3.

TEACHING STRATEGIES
Objective 1. Through group or independent study and using guiding questions developed by the teacher or through teacher-student interaction, students will develop a knowledge of the social patterns of several ethnic groups. Prepare a data retrieval chart such as the one shown here.

DATA RETRIEVAL CHART

Selected Aspects of Ethnic Social Patterns	Group 1	Group 2	Group 3	Group 4
Marriage and the Family				
Interpersonal Relationships				
Voluntary Associations				
Education				
Religion				

The preparation of this chart provides a means of consolidating the reports of small groups, summarizing a large body of information, organizing it into a manageable form for students, and facilitating learning activities such as comparisons and the development of generalizations.

References:
Amish—*186*
Chinese—*25, 244, 258*
Greeks—*383*
Hutterites—*389, 398*
Indians—*482*
Inuit—*514*
Italians—*567*
Mennonites—*186*
Portuguese—*717*

Objective 2. Divide students into groups, one group for each ethnic group studied in objective 1. Create a "family" within the group by assigning the roles of mother, father, grandparent(s), and one or more children. Have students discuss the role of each family member; then have the children move from one group to another. The parents and grandparents will explain the children's roles in their new family. Repeat several times. Begin a comparison of ethnic social patterns by discussing the students' experiences in the above activity. Continue the comparison by drawing upon the data gathered for objective 1.

Objective 3. Distribute a list of general statements about ethnic groups. Examples:
- Each ethnic group defines the role of children within the family.
- All non-European ethnic groups have experienced varying degrees of discrimination.
- Parents train their children according to their values.

Have students select those which are attributes of an ethnic group's social patterns. Using this exercise as a starting point, formulate, through class discussion, a definition of ethnic social patterns.

Objective 4. Working independently, students can prepare a written assignment on the social patterns of a group on the basis of the questions in objective 1 and the definition in objective 4. This assignment, as in Topic C, could be used in place of a test on this topic.

UNIT 2/IMMIGRATION

Topic A

Generalization: Immigrants have chosen to enter Canada for economic, political, religious, cultural, and personal reasons.

Teacher Reference: p. 13

OBJECTIVES
Students will be able to
1. (a) describe those economic, political, religious, and cultural characteristics of an immigrant group in its homeland relevant to understanding its emigration

(b) list and then rank, in terms of importance, the factors which motivated the particular group to immigrate to Canada
2. develop a generalization in response to the question: Why have immigrants chosen to enter Canada?
3. analyse a new reading according to objective 1

TEACHING STRATEGIES

Objective 1. Students can work independently or in groups, using teacher-developed guiding questions. These questions should reflect items *a* and *b* in the objective. The readings used for this objective should reflect a variety of motivations for immigrating.

References:
Americans—*179, 181*
British—*227, 228, 230, 235, 239*
Czechs—*271*
Doukhobors—*284*
Hutterites—*389*
Mennonites—*626*
Portuguese—*716*
Scots—*727*
Ukrainians—*747, 752*
Vietnamese—*759*

Objective 2. Students can now prepare a list of the factors which influenced the immigration of the groups represented in the case studies. Group and label these factors. After this task is completed, students should formulate a tentative generalization in response to the question in the objective. Obtain several generalizations from the class and test and revise them by examining them in terms of the data. The goal should be to develop a generalization with a broad range of applicability and accuracy.

Objective 3. Present students with one reading selected from the list provided for objective 1. Each student should write a short essay on that ethnic group, focussing on the topics suggested in objective 1. In addition, students should relate information about that ethnic group to the generalization developed for objective 2. Does the generalization apply in this case? If not, what changes should be made in it?

Topic B

Theme: There have been four major periods in the history of Canadian immigration, each with its own distinctive characteristics.

Teacher Reference: pp. 13-18

OBJECTIVES
Students will be able to
1. describe the history of each of the four periods of Canadian immigration in terms of the following topics: source and number of immigrants, their characteristics (e.g. education, occupation), their principal reasons for immigrating, settlement patterns, limitations on the entry of certain ethnic groups, and the relationship between emigration and immigration
2. compare and contrast periods two and four
3. identify, from readings, the arguments that favored ethnically restrictive immigration policies or were part of the controversy that surrounded a particular ethnic group
4. evaluate these arguments in terms of logic and factual accuracy
5. describe current immigration policies and regulations

6. develop hypotheses regarding the characteristics of immigrants entering Canada in the near future and future immigrant settlement patterns

TEACHING STRATEGIES

Objective 1. Through teacher lecture, independent work, or group work students will develop a knowledge of the four periods. Concentrate on the post-1967 phase of period four.

References: 25, 49, 84, 87, 107

Objective 2. Compare and contrast periods two and four. The comparison and contrast can begin with these two questions: What similarities and differences can be observed? How can these similarities and differences be explained?

References: 83, 84, 85, 93, 96, 98, 106, 110

Objective 3. Review Canada's ethnically restrictive immigration policies, objective 1. Have students study several of the readings listed below, noting the following:
— What arguments were used by some Canadians to support the idea that certain ethnic groups were undesirable immigrants?
— What attitudes were current in a particular period toward the group under study?
Be certain that students place each study in its historical context.

References:
Asians–*295*
Blacks–*217*
Chinese–*255, 256*
East Indians–*35*
Japanese–*578*
Orientals–*698*

Objective 4. Evaluate the arguments and claims regarding each ethnic group. The following questions can serve as a starting point:
— What facts were used by the proponents of these arguments to justify their views?
— Were there any bases in fact, in that period, to justify these views?
— What preconceived notions about particular ethnic groups were the bases of some of these claims?
— Ask students to place themselves in the shoes of someone living in that period. How would they have viewed these ethnic groups? Would they have supported these arguments?

Objective 5. Through teacher lecture or independent study students will develop a knowledge of current immigration policy and regulations.

References: 25, 53, 85

At the time of writing, the 1976 Immigration Act passed in 1977 had just been proclaimed (April 1978); as a result, there is a limited amount of literature available on it. For up-to-date information contact Employment and Immigration Canada, Information Services, 305 Rideau Street, Ottawa K1A 0J9.

Objective 6. Briefly lecture on the basic characteristics (ethnic origin, education, and occupation) of immigrants entering Canada in the 1970s and immigrant settlement patterns in the same time period. The process of hypothesis formation can begin with questions such as:

— What will be the characteristics of immigrants entering Canada in the next few years, given present trends?
— What will be the future trends in immigrant settlement patterns, given present trends?

References: 13, 25, 84, 85, 97, 110

Topic C

Theme: What has been the nature of the immigrant experience in Canada?

Teacher Reference: pp. 18, 19

OBJECTIVES
Students will be able to
1. describe the experiences of several immigrant groups
2. compare and contrast the experiences of several groups
3. develop generalizations about the immigrant experience
4. describe services provided for immigrants
5. evaluate the services provided at present

TEACHING STRATEGIES
Objective 1. Have students examine, either independently or in small groups, several of the readings suggested below. Guiding questions should either be presented by the teacher or developed through teacher-student interaction. The theme uniting these questions should be: What do we need to know in order to understand the immigrant experience in Canada? In addition, the possibility of students interviewing immigrants should be considered. A panel of guest speakers—all immigrants—would be a meaningful component of this study. For interviews or a panel, consider the suggestions about community studies made on pp. 35, 36. The preparation of a data retrieval chart (such as the one on p. 39) would help students clarify the information in preparation for objective 2.

References:
General works—*74, 78, 79, 81, 82, 86, 92, 105*
Americans—*180*
British—*237, 239*
Chinese—*255*
Croats—*268*
Czechs—*271*
Danes—*272*
Dutch—*288*
English—*299*
Germans—*373*
Icelanders—*401*
Italians—*571, 574*
Jews—*601, 609*
Portuguese—*719*
Ukrainians—*747, 752*
Vietnamese—*759*
West Indians—*765, 766*

Objective 2. The experiences of immigrant groups should be compared and contrasted. For example, compare and contrast the Chinese and Germans or the Czechs and Portuguese. In addition to identifying the similarities and differences in the experiences of the two groups, students should be encouraged to infer and discuss reasons for these similarities and differences.

Objective 3. Through class or small group discussion develop, test, and revise generalizations in response to two questions: What experiences have immigrants encountered? Why have the experiences of different immigrant groups varied so greatly? The focus could be on the post-World War II period or it could be expanded to include the whole range of Canadian immigration history.

Objective 4. Through teacher lecture or independent study, students will develop a knowledge of services provided for immigrants, concentrating on the purpose, scope, location, and sponsors of these services. In addition, students could investigate and report on any services for immigrants that are located in their own community.

References: 77, 85, 90, 99, 101

Objective 5. Evaluate the services which are available at present. Does it appear that they meet the needs of immigrants? Should these services be expanded? In what ways?

Topic D

Policy Issues: Is the policy embodied in the 1976 Immigration Act desirable? How should the Canadian government deal with the problem of illegal immigration?

Teacher Reference: pp. 17, 18

OBJECTIVES
Students will be able to
1. state and support a tentative position in response to the question on immigration policy
2. list a series of alternative immigration policies
3. predict the consequences of both the new immigration policy and alternative policies
4. assemble and evaluate evidence relevant to assessing the predicted consequences
5. establish criteria for determining the desirability of a policy
6. evaluate each policy according to its desirability
7. develop a personal position on the issue
8. develop a personal position on the issue of illegal immigration

TEACHING STRATEGIES
Objective 1. Clarify the purpose of this topic with students. Review the 1976 Immigration Act. Have students write a paragraph stating a preliminary position in response to the first issue.

Objective 2. Students will be better able to evaluate the desirability of the 1976 Immigration Act if they can compare it with alternative policies. For this reason, present the four policy options outlined in the Green Paper. Encourage students to suggest other possible immigration policies.

References: 84, 85, 97

Objective 3. Have students predict consequences of the 1976 Immigration Act and each of the alternative policies under consideration. Ensure that all terms being used are clearly understood. For example, do all students understand terms such as "quotas" and phrases such as "needs of our economy"?

Objective 4. Evaluate, in light of available information, the consequences predicted above. Incorporate data from Topics A-C and research sources. Discuss with students the types of information being used to evaluate the consequences.
— Is it opinion, inference, fact, or value judgment?
— Are the opinions and inferences based on factual evidence or prejudices and biases?
— What kinds of information are most relevant here?
— Are some of the predicted consequences highly unlikely based on the available information?
— Does the information suggest consequences in addition to others already listed?

References: 24, 84, 85, 86, 95, 102, 110

As a part of this research students could conduct interviews to measure the attitude and policy preferences of people in their community. The interviews should be highly structured and based on questions developed in class. If each student interviewed one adult family member and two non-family members, then a sample of about 100 interviewees would result. By assisting students in deciding who they will interview, teachers can ensure that the community survey will be somewhat representative. In addition, this process would incorporate the important social science concept of sampling. After the results have been tabulated by the class, discuss them, using questions similar to those in the above paragraph.

Objective 5. Before determining the desirability of a possible policy, students should establish criteria for determining desirability. These criteria will take the form of value judgments. Examples:
- Any immigration policy should relate to the needs of the Canadian economy.
- Any policy should respect the desire of established immigrants to sponsor immediate family members as immigrants.

Have students identify the values fundamental to each of the value statements they make.

Objective 6. Apply the criteria to the consequences of each alternative policy. In light of the criteria, how desirable is each alternative policy? Have students rank each policy according to its desirability.

Objective 7. Students can now prepare an essay on the issue: "Is the policy embodied in the 1976 Immigration Act desirable?" Their essay should include the predicted consequences of this policy, relevant data for assessing the consequences, their personal criteria for determining desirability, and a statement on the policy's desirability. If this policy is not desirable, what policy should Canada adopt?

Objective 8. Present students with one reading dealing with the problem of illegal immigration. Discuss questions such as:
— Who are illegal immigrants?
— Why do they enter Canada illegally?
— What is their life like in Canada?
— What happens to them when they are caught?

After examining the nature of the problem, have students prepare a personal position on the policy issue. Use a modified form of the approach outlined in objectives 1-7.

References: 75, 86, 91, 100

UNIT 3/INTERETHNIC RELATIONS

Topic A

Generalization: The relationship between an ethnic group and one or both of Canada's dominant communities can be located on a continuum ranging from complete segregation to group assimilation.

Teacher Reference: pp. 19, 20, 21

OBJECTIVES
Students will be able to
1. describe the relationship between an ethnic group and one or both of Canada's dominant communities, using teacher-developed guiding questions
2. locate the different types of relationships on a continuum and label each point on the continuum
3. develop and revise a generalization in response to the question: Why has there been such diversity in the types of relationships between individual ethnic groups and the larger society?
4. define integration and cultural and structural assimilation
5. state a personal position on a policy issue

TEACHING STRATEGIES
Objective 1. Divide the class into small groups. Assign to each group one or more readings. Each group can prepare a report for class presentation, using the guiding questions given below as a starting point. As each group presents its report, the class can prepare a data retrieval chart similar to the one on p. 39. The topics for the vertical column can be developed from the guiding questions. No readings illustrating relationships between Canada's two dominant communities have been included here because this topic is too complex to be treated in this manner. In addition, it is assumed that students will have a much fuller exposure to this topic in history courses, units on national unity, or both. However, readings about either English or French minorities in provinces dominated by the other language group have been included because they clearly relate to the theme under study and the approach being used.

GUIDING QUESTIONS
1. How does the dominant community view Group X?
2. How do members of Group X view the dominant community?
3. Do members of Group X have economic, educational, political, and residential opportunities equal to those of the rest of society?
4. Do members of Group X and the larger society interact freely on a social basis?
5. Do members of Group X want to participate fully in the larger society?
6. Do members of Group X see their position as desirable or undesirable? Explain.
7. If conflict has developed between Group X and the dominant community, why did it develop and what was the nature of the conflict?
8. Have members of Group X changed in order to become members of the larger society?
9. Do some or all members of Group X identify with the dominant society?
10. Does the larger society exert pressures on Group X to become more like the majority society?

References:
Blacks—*25, 205, 213*

Chinese—*244, 246, 259*
English Quebeckers—*229, 231, 234, 238*
Franco-Manitobans—*312, 360*
Francophones outside Quebec—*330, 331*
Germans—*25*
Hutterites—*24, 389, 391*
Indians—*412, 416, 430, 440*
Italians—*25, 567, 568, 573*
Japanese—*25, 581, 583, 585, 595*
Métis—*659*
Native Peoples—*668, 674, 689*
Orientals—*699, 703*

Objective 2. Explain concepts of total segregation and group assimilation. Identify these as two points on a continuum of interethnic relations. Have students locate case studies on such a continuum. Discuss appropriate labels for each point.

Objective 3. Before asking students to state a generalization in response to the question posed in the objective, have them list, group, and label all the factors which have affected interethnic relations in Canada. Have students write a tentative generalization, select several of these, and discuss them. After that, have students revise, if necessary, their own generalizations, bearing in mind the class discussion.

Objective 4. Explain concepts of integration and cultural and structural assimilation. How are these illustrated by the readings?

Objective 5. Explore the following policy issue: Should ethnic groups in Canadian society be encouraged to assimilate, integrate, or segregate? Follow the approach, as outlined on p. 45, of stating a tentative position, predicting consequences, assessing consequences, defining criteria, evaluating each policy alternative, and stating a final personal position.

Topic B

Theme: Social and cultural change

Teacher Reference: pp. 21, 22

OBJECTIVES
Students will be able to
1. discuss, on the basis of participation in or observation of role-playing activities, their feelings about and reactions to the social and cultural change affecting a particular ethnic group
2. describe the social and cultural changes which have taken place among ethnic groups in Canada
3. identify the causes of the changes
4. state a definition of social and cultural change
5. develop and revise generalizations in response to the questions: Why has social and cultural change occurred among ethnic groups in Canada? What have been the effects of this social and cultural change?
6. compare the Amish or Hutterites with another ethnic group in terms of the degree of social and cultural change which has taken place

7. develop and revise a generalization in response to the following question: Why have the Amish or Hutterites been relatively unaffected by social and cultural change in comparison with other ethnic groups?

TEACHING STRATEGIES

Objective 1. Create role-playing activities around one or more of the following situations:

● Maria is the sixteen-year-old daughter of Portuguese immigrants who arrived in Canada eight years ago. She has excelled academically, mastered English beautifully, and developed a circle of non-Portuguese friends in her high school. Impressed by the career opportunities open to women in Canada, Maria hopes to be a lawyer or engineer. Because of parental restrictions, Maria has never attended a dance or had a date. She is under a lot of pressure from her school friends to join them in these activities. One of the boys in the school invites her to the dance of the year. When her friends hear this, they increase their pressure on Maria to prevail upon her parents to allow her to go. Role-play the scene in her home that night as Maria determinedly seeks permission to attend the dance.

Reference: 720

● Ten years ago Teya and Satya were married in India. Their marriage had been arranged by their families and they had only met on several occasions before the wedding ceremony. Teya and Satya immigrated to Canada two months after their marriage. They now have two sons, aged eight and four. Because they have worked hard and prospered in Canada, they were able to bring Satya's widowed mother to Canada to live with them.

Lately, Satya has frequently asked her husband if they could both work together to plan the family's budget. Teya's reply has been an authoritative "no." Sometimes Satya wishes her husband would learn from North American men; it would be so pleasant if they could take part in some social activities together. Satya also has been considering getting a job; after all, she has her capable mother with her to care for the children. Teya has not been receptive to the idea, saying that a woman's place is in the home. Satya takes the initiative and obtains a job as a filing clerk in a large office. Role-play the discussion between Teya and Satya which follows her announcement that she has a job.

Reference: 297

● Michael Immaroitug, an eighteen-year-old Inuit, has spent the last ten years attending a residential school in Inuvik. While there, he lived with southern comforts, learned to speak fluent English, and became thoroughly immersed in the "white man's" culture. He spent only two months of each year with his parents. Now that he has finished his schooling, Michael has returned home for a short visit before heading back to Inuvik in hopes of finding a job. The rest of his family, including three young children, are leaving their settlement to move back to the land and live as the Inuit once did. They are tired of welfare, and the alcoholism and idleness of their settlement. They see it as a difficult adjustment but necessary for them to rebuild their self-respect. Michael scorns the idea and dreams of a job in Inuvik where the money and good times are. Role-play a family discussion in which Michael's parents try to persuade him to make the transition with them.

Reference: 542

Follow up the role playing by discussing questions such as:
— What has happened in the lives of Maria, Satya, and Michael?
— Why have these changes taken place?
— Why did Maria's parents, Teya, and Michael's parents react the way they did?
— How would you feel if you were Maria, Satya, or Michael?
— How would you feel if you were Maria's parents, Teya, or Michael's parents?

Objective 2. Through group or independent study and using guiding questions developed by the teacher or through teacher-student interaction, students will develop a knowledge of the changes taking place among several ethnic groups. Prepare a data retrieval chart such as the one illustrated on p. 39.

References:
Danes–*25*
Doukhobors–*276*
French Canadians outside Quebec–*25, 312, 330*
Indians–*25*
Inuit–*25, 522, 542, 558, 559*
Jews–*619*
Portuguese–*25, 720*
Ukrainians–*748*

Objective 3. Ask students to identify the causes of the changes examined in each reading. If no causes are given, students will then have to make inferences. Group the causes and label them. Have causes varied from one group to another? Why?

Objective 4. Before asking students to define social and cultural change, review the concepts of ethnic culture and ethnic social patterns. Obtain several definitions, and test them in terms of specific data from the case studies. Create a comprehensive definition.

Objective 5. Have students write tentative generalizations in response to the questions in the objective. Before considering the second question, list and group the effects social and cultural change have had. Through class discussion develop and revise comprehensive generalizations.

Objectives 6 and 7. Examine either the Amish or Hutterites, using one of the readings listed below.
– Has social and cultural change occurred among these two groups? To what extent?
– What are their attitudes toward change?
– How do they try to prevent change? How successful are they?
Compare and contrast the groups studied in objective 2. Consider explanations for the similarities and differences identified.

References:
Amish–*23, 186*
Hutterites–*25, 389, 392, 397*

Develop a generalization in response to the question in the objective.

Topic C

Generalization: In any society where there is stratification based on ethnicity, there are ethnic minority groups.

Teacher Reference: pp. 9 to 10 and 22 to 23

OBJECTIVES
Students will be able to
1. describe the current or historical status, or both (educational, social, political, and economic), of an ethnic minority group
2. distinguish between "voluntary" and "involuntary" minority groups

3. develop and revise a generalization in response to each of the following questions: What distinguishes ethnic minority groups from other ethnic groups? Why are some ethnic groups minority groups while others are not?
4. describe the goals of a minority group
5. compare and contrast the goals of minority groups
6. develop and revise a generalization in response to the following question: What is the relationship between an ethnic group's minority status and its goals?
7. state a personal position on a policy issue

TEACHING STRATEGIES

Objective 1. Review the concept of ethnic minority group from Unit I, Topic B. Divide the class into small groups. Assign to each group one reading. Each group should prepare a report for class presentation based on teacher-developed guiding questions derived from the teacher reference section. As each group presents its report, the class can prepare a data retrieval chart similar to the one on p. 39. The topics for the vertical column can be developed from the guiding questions.

References:
Acadians–*303*
Amish–*184*
Blacks–*14, 196, 197, 200, 213, 218*
Chinese–*253*
Hutterites–*24, 389, 398*
Indians–*411, 431, 435, 436, 448, 463, 468, 478, 492*
Inuit–*531, 555*
Métis–*659, 665*
Native Peoples–*17, 694*

Objective 2. Tell students that the Hutterites and Amish are "voluntary" minority groups while the others are "involuntary" minority groups. What are the similarities and differences between the two types of minority groups? Why do these similarities and differences exist?

Objective 3. Indicate to students that the groups studied for objective 1 are minority groups while others studied earlier, such as Germans, Hungarians, and Scots, are not. Have students suggest as many differences as they can. Group these. Students are then ready to write a tentative answer to the first question in the objective. After that, discuss several of the students' generalizations and encourage them to revise their own, if necessary, based on the class discussion. Follow a similar strategy for the second question.

Objective 4. Have the small groups re-examine their case studies and identify the goals of the minority groups.
— How do they want to accomplish these goals?
— Will the English- or French-Canadian communities have to change policies and attitudes if the minority group is to achieve its goals?
— What is the group doing to accomplish its goals?
— Will assistance from either or both of the dominant communities be a necessary part of the process?
— Will the group still be a minority group when it accomplishes its goals?
— Will the group and the dominant society's attitudes toward each other change as the group achieves its goals?
— Will the group's perception of itself and its status change as it achieves its goals?

Objective 5. Before beginning the comparison and contrast, have students compile a list of the goals of all groups studied. What similarities and differences exist? What are some explanations for these similarities and differences?

Objective 6. Follow the same strategy as in objective 3.

Objective 7. Examine several of the following policy issues or others which have arisen during the study of this topic.
— Should ethnic groups with pacifist religious beliefs be exempted from military service?
— Should the Canadian government recognize the land claims of the Native Peoples?
— Should educational systems be changed to reflect the concerns of the Native Peoples?
— Should Hutterites have complete freedom in expanding their land holdings?
— Do Canadians, through their governments or individually, have a responsibility to assist minority groups in preserving their cultures?
— Do Canadians, through their governments or individually, have a responsibility to actively work toward eliminating the barriers faced by minority groups?
Follow the strategy described on p. 45.

Topic D

Theme: Ethnocentrism, stereotypes, racism, prejudice, and discrimination.

Teacher Reference: pp. 23, 24, 25

OBJECTIVES
Students will be able to
1. discuss, on the basis of participation in, or observation of, role-playing activities, their feelings about and reactions to the experiences of individuals victimized by prejudice and discrimination
2. define ethnocentrism, stereotypes, racism, prejudice, and discrimination
3. describe the prejudice and discrimination being directed against a particular ethnic group
4. develop and revise generalizations in response to the following questions: Why do some Canadians discriminate and hold prejudiced beliefs and attitudes against other Canadians of different backgrounds? What are the effects of prejudice and discrimination on the victims?
5. describe and evaluate what is being done to overcome prejudice and discrimination
6. suggest ways in which prejudice and discrimination can be eliminated at a personal and a societal level.

TEACHING STRATEGIES
Teachers must be aware of the dangers associated with this topic if there are minority group children in the class. *The tendency to dive in and ask Johnny to "tell it like it is" must be avoided.* Understandably, most minority children will feel self-conscious in this situation and will deny any unpleasant experiences, out of a desire to be accepted.

There are no easy solutions, but one approach might be to speak to the minority group child or children, on an individual basis, outside of the classroom situation, and discuss the upcoming study of prejudice and discrimination. Emphasize that the long-range goal is the elimination of the problem, not the further isolation of those who are labelled as being different. The students could be encouraged to speak about their experiences and feelings if they feel comfortable about doing so.

In addition, the teacher should speak to the natural leaders in the class and ask for their assistance in creating a sensitive classroom climate. A similar strategy might work with any "Archie Bunkers" in the class.

The following role-playing activities and follow-up discussions should alert students to the feelings of the victimized and, as a result, help create a supportive classroom climate.

Objective 1. Create role-playing activities around the following situations:
- Michael Brown is in his third year of school. He is the only Black child in his class. His family lives in a predominantly white suburb of a large Canadian city. During the last few months, Michael's mother has noticed that he is sometimes unhappy when he arrives home from school. One day he seems particularly glum, and while he is having an after-school snack he asks his mother what "jungle bunnies" and "tar babies" are. Role-play the conversation that follows between mother and son regarding the discrimination Michael has been encountering at school.
- While attending university, Anne Simpson began to date Johnny Littlefeathers. Anne did not tell her parents about her Indian boyfriend until they were considering marriage. To date, Anne's parents have firmly but calmly discouraged her from dating an Indian. Finally, Anne and Johnny decide to be married and announce their plans to her parents during an evening visit. Role-play the discussion that ensues.
- Three grade eight boys have been harassing Amrik Singh, a Sikh boy. The harassment gradually increases from name calling to pranks to shoving in the halls. This comes to a head in the locker room when the bullies grab Amrik's turban. At that moment, the physical education teacher enters the locker room and puts a stop to the incident. The three boys are referred to the guidance counsellor who, after consultation with Amrik, decides that the culprits should "talk out" the situation with their victim. Role-play the discussion in the counsellor's office.

Follow up the role-playing activities by discussion questions such as:
— How does it feel to be the victim of discrimination?
— How would you react if you were Michael, Johnny, or Amrik?
— What are the reasons for the discrimination exhibited in each situation?

Objective 2. Explain the five terms based on the material in the teacher reference section. Begin a discussion by asking students to react to some of the stereotypes of teenagers. From this point discuss the validity of a statement such as "All Bunwaldis are smelly, pushy, and rude."
— What stereotypes of ethnic groups exist in our society?
— How do stereotypes of teenagers or ethnic groups hurt the people who believe them and the people described by them?
— How do stereotypes ignore individual differences within any group of people?

An ethnocentric person can be described as being blinded by his own culture. What does this mean? How does an ethnocentric individual react to a new neighbor of a different cultural background or another country with a different culture? Does ethnocentrism lead to prejudice and discrimination?

Discuss examples of prejudice and discrimination which students suggest. Why do prejudice and discrimination exist?

Objective 3. Have students, working independently or in small groups, examine several of the readings listed below. There are four main questions that are important here:
— What is the nature of the prejudice and discrimination directed against a particular group?
— Is there any evidence to explain why that group has been singled out?
— How do the victims react?

— Is anything being done to solve the problem?

This would be an appropriate time for further community research, with leaders of ethnic communities or organizations acting as guest speakers or resource people for student interviewers.

References:
Blacks—*44, 45, 50, 203, 204*
East Indians—*292, 294, 296, 298*
Indians—*431, 433, 475*
Japanese—*586*
Jews—*616*
Native Peoples—*687, 694*
South Asians—*734*

Objective 4. Through class discussion develop a list of the reasons for prejudice and discrimination, based on the readings studied in the previous objective. Follow up with further work on the reasons for prejudice and discrimination, based on a teacher lecture or on student research.

References: 25, 36, 46, 47, 50, 59, 67

Having done that, proceed with the generalization-development process.

List the effects of prejudice and discrimination from both the readings studied in objective 3 and the references cited for this objective. Group and label these and then proceed with the usual generalization-development process.

Objective 5. Examine the activities of the federal Canadian Human Rights Commission and several of the provincial human rights commissions. In addition, examine several pieces of human rights legislation.

Reference: 48

Further information can be obtained from the federal commission in Ottawa and the commission in each province.

What activities, sponsored by governments, voluntary groups, or both, are being carried out in your community?

Evaluate the effectiveness of the human rights commissions and local programs. What criteria should be used in such an evaluation? What data are necessary?

Objective 6. Encourage students to seriously consider if they hold any ethnic prejudices, and, if so, how they can change them. Discuss:
— Does a child begin to develop stereotypes about Indians by playing cowboys and Indians?
— Do ethnic jokes reflect prejudice and discrimination?
— How would you react if your son (or daughter) announced that he (she) was going to marry someone of another race?
— Does the popularity of Archie Bunker reflect people's willingness to identify with a prejudiced person?
— Does television perpetuate ethnic stereotypes?
— If an acquaintance said "Indians are nothing but lazy drunken nogoods living off hard-working taxpayers' money," how would you react? Would you agree, disagree, or say nothing?
— If an East Indian family moved in next door would you make the same friendly overtures to that family as to a European family?

Following this discussion of prejudice and discrimination at a personal level, examine alternative ways of eliminating the problem at the societal level.

UNIT 4/THE IMPACT OF ETHNIC DIVERSITY

Teacher Reference: pp. 25, 26, 27

OBJECTIVES
Students will be able to
1. define ethnic mosaic
2. identify relationships between ethnic origin and occupational levels, given empirical data
3. develop and explain inferences regarding this data
4. evaluate the validity of the ethnic mosaic image
5. state a conclusion in response to the following question: Do ethnic groups preserve and evolve distinctive cultural patterns?
6. identify (from readings), given teacher-prepared guiding questions, information relevant to assessing the impact of ethnic diversity on Canadian society, culture, politics, and economics
7. develop conclusions based on the data gathered for objective 6.

TEACHING STRATEGIES
Objective 1. Explain ethnic mosaic. Point out the purpose of this unit and explain the two ways, from p. 25, of determining the validity of the ethnic mosaic image. Stress that a true ethnic mosaic would mean that ethnic groups would preserve and develop unique cultural patterns while integrating fully into all sectors of Canadian life, if they so wished.

Objective 2. There are several ways of measuring integration but, at the high school level, the following exercise should be sufficient to alert students to the relationship between ethnic origin and degree of integration. The relationships indicated in this exercise are typical, with some exceptions, of those to be found in the political, cultural, and social spheres of Canadian life. In addition, any further exploration would, for high school students, be more tedious than productive.

Explain over- and under-representation. Present students with tables from the reference cited below. Using the 1961 data, determine the degree of a group's over- and underrepresentation in each occupational category. This could best be accomplished by group work, each group analysing one ethnic group. After the group work, compile a table showing the results of the analysis.

As of 1961, what is the pattern for each ethnic group? French Canadians constitute one of Canada's two dominant communities. Comment on their patterns of occupational representation in light of this fact.
Reference: 49, pp. 268-71 or 172, p. 87

Objective 3. Ask students to explain, by means of inferences, the reasons for the under- and over-representation found in the above activity. Incorporate information and concepts from earlier units.

Objective 4. Do the data studied for objective 2 indicate that all ethnic groups are integrated into the occupational sphere of Canadian life? On the basis of conclusions developed for objectives 2 and 4, is Canada a true ethnic mosaic? What image might better describe Canada?

Objective 5. The best approach to this topic is teacher-directed discussion of readings examined in other units. Review six to eight readings, representing a broad range of

ethnic groups. Explain that the ethnic mosaic image implies that ethnic cultures will grow and develop, suggesting something quite different from the preservation of a few dances, songs, customs, and so on.
— To what extent is each group preserving and developing a distinctive culture?
— Can a person who is basically English Canadian in culture maintain a strong identification with his ethnic origin?
— Will the children and grandchildren of today's urban immigrant communities preserve and develop distinctive cultures, or will their link with their heritage be one of identification rather than cultural distinctiveness?

Objective 6. Using guiding questions developed from those on p. 28, have students, working in small groups, investigate one or more readings selected from the list given below. Again, the construction of a data retrieval chart would be a useful way of summarizing the information.

References:
General topics—*41, 49, 55, 56, 57, 60, 69, 129*   Italians—*568*
Chinese—*261, 264*   Jews—*607, 613*
Czechs—*270*   Inuit—*517, 518, 528*
Germans—*371, 373, 380*   Native Peoples—*694*
Icelanders—*400, 403*   Scots—*729*
                                                   Ukrainians—*740*

Objective 7. Discuss:
— What has been the impact of ethnic diversity on Canadian society, culture, politics, and economics?
— Has the English-Canadian community been influenced by the other cultures in Canada?
— Has ethnic diversity had as much impact on the English-Canadian community as Americanization and urbanization?
— Why hasn't the English-Canadian community been more influenced by ethnic diversity?
Caution students to regard all answers to these questions as tentative because the case studies do not provide a sufficient data base for conclusive answers.

UNIT 5/SHOULD CANADA SEEK TO BECOME A TRULY MULTICULTURAL, BILINGUAL SOCIETY?

Teacher Reference: pp. 27 to 29

OBJECTIVES
Students will be able to
1. describe the policy and programs of multiculturalism and bilingualism
2. explain the historical origins of the multiculturalism and bilingualism policies
3. identify the values fundamental to both policies
4. explain four model social and cultural policies
5. develop a personal position on two policy issues

TEACHING STRATEGIES
Objective 1. Introduce this unit with a teacher lecture or independent student work on the policies and programs.
— What goals are stated in the policies?
— What rationale or justification supports each policy?
— What programs have been established?

References: 25, 107, 118, 125, 139, 144, 313, 326

Objective 2. Lecture briefly on the origins of both policies. Relate the history of both policies to the findings and recommendations of the Royal Commission on Bilingualism and Biculturalism.

References: 25, 121, 122, 125, 139, 144, 326

Objective 3. Present students with extracts from official statements relating to both policies. What values are fundamental to each policy? For example, what value underlies the following statement "the government will assist members of all cultural groups to overcome cultural barriers to full participation in Canadian society"?

Objective 4. Lecture on the four models. Stress that they are models, not descriptive statements about Canada's society, past or present. Encourage students to make inferences about the nature of Canadian society if one of the four models were adopted as a policy goal.

Objective 5. Explore the following policy issue: Should Canada seek to become a truly multicultural, bilingual society? Follow the approach, as described on pp. 44-46, of stating a tentative position, predicting consequences, assessing consequences, defining criteria, evaluating each policy alternative, and stating a final personal position.

References: 25, 117, 120, 123, 124, 126, 129, 130, 131, 136, 138, 326

CHAPTER 4

A Selected Bibliography of Instructional Materials

Introduction

The bibliography in this chapter lists instructional materials, both print and audio-visual, suitable for use in grades 5-12. Some general comments about the bibliography are in order.

1. This bibliography is designed to be primarily a service bibliography for teachers rather than a research one; however, references to other bibliographies have been cited to provide starting points for further research for those teachers and students desiring to do so.

2. The references cited in this bibliography have been limited to those most suitable, in terms of reading and interest level, for use in grades 5 to 12. Each print item has been classified according to reading level. Five reading levels have been designated:
- A—grades 5-6
- B—grades 7-8
- C—grades 9-10
- D—grades 11-12
- E—advanced

The use of reading and interest level as key criteria in the selection process has meant that many items have been rejected that would be of little value in the classroom. Nevertheless, references to major scholarly works have been included for the use of teachers and advanced students.

3. All print items have been examined to determine their suitability according to the criteria outlined above.

4. The items have been divided into two major categories—general works and works on individual ethnic groups—and then further subdivided according to topic or ethnic group.

5. A cursory survey of this bibliography will reveal that the number of references varies greatly from one ethnic group to another. This reflects the general state of the literature, especially in mass market magazines.

6. Wherever possible, references have been selected to provide a broad regional representation. Because of this aim, references to articles in periodicals such as *Toronto Life, BC Studies,* and *Axiom* have been included, even if these periodicals are not likely to be found in school libraries outside their regions.

7. All books listed are in print and have been verified either in *Canadian Books in Print 1976*, or with the publisher. As a general rule, only periodical items published since the late 1960s have been included. Again, this decision was based on a desire to make the bibliography usable by listing only those items that can be either purchased or found in school and public libraries.

8. Addresses of publishers and distributors have been provided at the end of the bibliography.

9. References to newspapers and magazines published by ethnic organizations and government agencies have also been included. Their addresses are also provided.

10. Prices have not been included because they soon become out-of-date; however, items that are available free of charge have been noted.

General Works

BIBLIOGRAPHIES
(Bibliographies on individual ethnic groups and topics are listed with the group or topic.)

1   Canada. Department of Labour. Economics and Research Branch. *Discrimination in Employment: A Selected Annotated Bibliography.* Compiled by Karen Herring. Ottawa: 1970, 65 pp., free.

2   Canada. Department of the Secretary of State. *Human Rights Research in Canada: A Bibliography.* Compiled by Robert L. James. Ottawa: 1970, 64 pp., paper, free.

3   *Canadian Ethnic Studies.* Semiannual.

Each issue contains book reviews, film reviews, bibliographies, and/or biographical essays.

4   *Communique,* vol. 3, no. 1, 1976. Special Issue: Multiculturalism.

A bibliography, 65 pp.

5   McLeod, Keith A., comp. *A Select Bibliography on Ethnicity and Multiculturalism for High Schools.* Toronto: K. A. McLeod, 1974, 24 pp., mimeo.

6   McLeod, Keith A., ed., and McQuillan, Barry H., comp. *A Resource List of Multi-Media Materials on Ethnicity and Multi-culturalism.* Toronto: K. A. McLeod, 1974, 34 pp., mimeo.

7   Ontario. Department of the Provincial Secretary and Citizenship. *Canadian Ethnic Groups Bibliography: A Selected Bibliography of Ethno-Cultural Groups and the Province of Ontario.* Compiled by Andrew Gregorovich. Toronto: 1972, 208 pp., paper. Distributor: Government of Ontario Bookstore.

8   Ontario. Ministry of Education and Ministry of Culture and Recreation. *Resource List for a Multicultural Society.* Compiled by Janet Maxwell, B. Rubess, I. Sabanskis, and D. Todd. Toronto: 1976, 626 pp., paper. Distributor: Ministry of Government Services, Printing Services Branch.

In addition to listing items on ethnic groups in Canada, considerable emphasis is placed on references relating to the groups' heritages and homelands. A service bibliography for educators.

9   Ontario. Ministry of Labour. Research Branch. *Minority Groups in Metropolitan Toronto Number 2: A Supplement to the 1973 Bibliography.* Toronto: 1975, 48 pp., free.

10   *Quill and Quire.* Seventeen issues a year.

Lists and reviews new and forthcoming books. Useful for updating existing bibliographies and resource lists.

11   Robinson, Paul. *After Survival: A Teacher's Guide to Canadian Resources.* Toronto: Peter Martin Associates, 1977, 329 pp., paper.

This bibliography of instructional materials contains two chapters with ethnic themes. These are "Indian-Inuit-Métis" and "Ukrainians and Other Unknown Canadians."

INSTRUCTIONAL MATERIALS
(Books, periodicals, and audio-visual materials prepared specifically for classroom use. Materials on only one ethnic group or topic are listed with the references on that group or topic.)

12   Andrew, Robert, and Mason, Trisha. *We Are Their Children: Ethnic Portraits of British Columbia.* Vancouver: Commcept, 1977, 162 pp., paper.

Case studies of nine ethnic groups and nine regions in British Columbia. The former center around individuals and families. There is an accompanying teachers' guide. B

13   Bavington, Jack; Lithwick, B.; Sproule, W.; and Thompson, N. *Cultures in Canada.* Toronto: Maclean-Hunter Learning Materials, 1976, 154 pp., paper.

Examines the concept culture, ethnic cultures in Canada, immigration, the immigrant experience, and interethnic relations. C

14   Bowles, R. P.; Hanley, J. L.; Hodgins, B. W.; and Rawlyk, G. A. *Social Change.* Scarborough, Ont.: Prentice-Hall of Canada, 1972, 209 pp., paper.

This book of readings includes sections on Doukhobors (Sons of Freedom), Blacks, Indians, Métis (Riel Rebellion), and French Canadians (separatists). C

15   *Canada and the World.* October 1976. Special Issue: Multicultural Heritage.

One article on the federal policy of multiculturalism and five articles on ethnic groups: Chinese, Doukhobors, Germans, Irish, and Italians. B

16   *The Canadian Mosaic* (kit). Toronto: Moreland-Latchford, 1975. 8 filmstrips, 8 cassettes, and 1 teacher's guide.

One filmstrip on each of the following topics: mosaic Canada, British Canadians, French Canadians, Native Canadians, European Canadians, Black Canadians, Chinese and Japanese Canadians, and cultures in conflict. Primarily a historical approach.

17   Doughty, Howard A.; Skidmore, D. R.; King, A. J. C.; and Munro, I. R. *Canadian Studies: Culture and Country.* Toronto: Wiley, 1976, 283 pp., cloth.

An ethnic studies text composed of six sections: introduction to the study of ethnicity and immigration, Native Peoples, British, French, eight other ethnic groups and issues associated with ethnic diversity. C

18 *Ethnic Culture in Canada* (kit). Scarborough: ETHOS, 1974. 6 filmstrips, 6 cassettes, and 3 reading scripts.

"the cultural, social, and urban effects of ethnic groups on Canadian life."

19 *The Peoples of Canada: Our Multicultural Heritage* (kit). Scarborough: Prentice-Hall Media, 1976. 3 filmstrips, 3 cassettes, and 1 teacher's guide.

Canada's multicultural heritage is approached from a historical perspective, beginning with the arrival of the Native Peoples in North America and concluding with contemporary concerns such as land claims, language policy, and immigration policy.

20 Remnant, Robert; Wood, Dean; Longarini, Dave; and Peck, Gary. *Canadian Multiculturalism: Values and Concepts.* 1977, 118 pp.

An eight- to ten-week unit for grades 9-10, the product of a curriculum development project sponsored by the Canada Studies Foundation.

21 Riddell, Barry; Sproule, W.; Thompson, N.; Lynch, J.; and Hubbard, K. *Minority Groups.* Toronto: Maclean-Hunter Learning Materials, 1971, 36 pp., paper.

Prepared for classroom use. C

22 Sheffe, Norman, ed. *Many Cultures, Many Heritages.* Toronto: McGraw-Hill Ryerson, 1975, 546 pp., cloth.

A text with chapters on the Blacks, British, French, Germans, Italians, Japanese, Jews, Native Peoples, Scandinavians, and Ukrainians. The approach is primarily historical. Each chapter was prepared by a different author(s). C

23 Skeoch, Alan, and Smith, Tony, eds. *Canadians and Their Society.* Toronto: McClelland and Stewart, 1973, 228 pp., paper.

This book of readings includes articles on Doukhobors, Indians, French Canadians, Blacks, Inuit, Italians, Mennonites, and racial stereotypes. D

24 Troper, Harold, and Palmer, Lee. *Issues in Cultural Diversity.* Toronto: Ontario Institute for Studies in Education, 1976, 130 pp., paper.

A series of case studies about minority groups. Each study consists of a basic reading, questions, and analogies. C

25 Wood, Dean, and Remnant, Robert. *The People We Are: Canada's Multicultural Society.* Agincourt, Ont.: Gage, forthcoming (1979), 320 pp., cloth.

A thematic, interdisciplinary text for ethnic studies. Contains chapters on the following topics: ethnic cultures and social patterns, immigration, interethnic relations, change, prejudice and discrimincation, impact of ethnic diversity, and the policy and programs of multiculturalism. C

COMPREHENSIVE WORKS
(Books and periodicals with separate sections on three or more ethnic groups.)

26   Beattie, C., and Crysdale, S., eds. *Sociology Canada: Readings.* Toronto: Butterworth, 1974, 504 pp., paper.

A book of readings with articles on Italians, Greeks, Inuit, Indians, French, and Hutterites. E

27   Blishen, Bernard R.; Jones, Frank E.; Naegele, Kaspar D.; and Porter, John, eds. *Canadian Society: Sociological Perspectives.* 3d ed. Toronto: Macmillan, 1968, cloth.

A collection of 53 scholarly articles; one-third of these have ethnic studies themes. D and E

28   Canada. Department of the Secretary of State. *The Canadian Family Tree.* Ottawa: Queen's Printer, 1967, 354 pp., paper and cloth.

The history, customs, organizations, and contributions of 49 different ethnic groups. This volume is presently out of print (1978), but there are plans to publish a revised edition.

29   *Canadian Ethnic Studies.* Semiannual.

This journal is published by the Canadian Ethnic Studies Association. D and E

30   Davis, Morris, and Krauter, Joseph R. *The Other Canadians: Profiles of Six Minorities.* Toronto: Methuen, 1971, 132 pp., paper.

The history of seven ethnic minority groups: Indians, Inuit, Blacks, Chinese, Japanese, Doukhobors, and Hutterites. A concluding chapter examines several themes related to minority status. C

31   *Encyclopedia Canadiana,* 1972.

There are articles, of varying length and quality, on approximately 50 ethnic groups. C

32   *Heritage.* Bimonthly, free.

The articles in *Heritage*, published by Alberta Culture, focus on Alberta's history and ethnic groups. B

33   Ishwaran, K. *The Canadian Family: Revised.* Toronto: Holt, Rinehart and Winston, 1976, 705 pp., paper and cloth.

Scholarly articles on marriage and the family among the Sikhs, Lebanese, Muslims, Indians, Inuit, Jews, Japanese, Italians, Hutterites, Dutch, and French Canadians. D and E

34   Markotic, Vladimir, and Petrunic, T. *Ethnic Directory of Canada.* Calgary: Western Publishers, 1975, paper.

A listing, complete with addresses, of ethnic organizations, churches, restaurants, businesses, and schools. The directory is organized according to province, city or town, and ethnic group.

35   Minghi, Julian V., ed. *Peoples of the Living Land: Geography of Cultural Diversity in British Columbia.* Vancouver: Tantalus Research, 1972, paper.

Three papers on the Chinese, Japanese, and East Indian communities in British Columbia. D

36 Morton, Tom, and McBride, John. *Look Again: The Process of Prejudice and Discrimination.* Vancouver: Commcept, 1977, 90 pp., paper.

A very useful unit text focussing on the following topics: perceptions and our patterns of thinking, prejudice, stereotypes, discrimination, causes of prejudice and discrimination, and overcoming the problem. There is also a valuable *Teachers' Resource Book.* C

37 *The Newcomers . . . Inhabiting a New Land* (motion pictures). Toronto: Imperial Oil, 1977-79. (16mm, color)

A series of seven 60-minute films commissioned by Imperial Oil. Each film portrays a different ethnic group at a different period in Canadian history. The company plans to make the films available for widespread educational use. Contact the Public Affairs Department regarding availability in a particular area.

38 Ontario. Ministry of Culture and Recreation. Multicultural Development Branch. *Ethnic Composition of Ontario 1971.* Toronto: 1976, n. p., mimeo, free.

Useful reference source for community studies.

39. ———. *Ethnocultural Directory of Ontario.* Toronto: 1977, 110 pp., mimeo, free.

A listing of ethnic organizations.

TOPICS IN ETHNIC STUDIES
(Prejudice, discrimination, interethnic relations, folklore, crafts, etc.)

40 A. Z. K./I. J. C. [Kerekes, Andrew Z., and Collins, Ian J.] "Government Action to Secure Human Rights." *Quarterly of Canadian Studies for the Secondary School*, vol. 2, no. 4, 1973, pp. 224-29. D

41 August, Raymond. "Babeling Beaver Hunts for Home Fire: The Place of Ethnic Literature in Canadian Culture." *Canadian Forum*, August 1974, pp. 8-13. D

42 Bella, Leslie. "Racial Tension in a Core Neighborhood." *Canadian Welfare*, August 1971, pp. 8-10.

Interethnic relations among Indians, Métis, Ukrainians, and Poles. C

43 *Bilingualism: Rags and Riches* (audiotape). Toronto: Canadian Broadcasting Corporation, 1969. (60 min., reel and cassette)

An examination of bilingualism in its larger meaning, not just English-French bilingualism. Specific attention is paid to bilingualism among ethnic group members.

44 Brown, Dick. "The Coloring of Canada." *Quest*, September/October 1975, pp. 24-28.

Racism in Canada. C

45   Brown, Rose Tanner. "Racism in Canada. So You Think It's Just a Few Punks in Subway Stations." *Last Post*, April 1977, pp. 28-37. C

46   Canada. Department of the Secretary of State. *Prejudice and Discrimination: A Study Guide.* Ottawa: 1975, 90 pp., paper, free. C

47   Canada. Labour Canada. Fair Employment Practices. *Toward Understanding: Prejudice, Discrimination.* Ottawa: n.d., 68 pp., free.

Five short, readable essays on the nature and causes of prejudice and discrimination. C

48   Canada. Labour Canada. Legislative Research. *Human Rights in Canada 1975: Legislation and Decisions.* By Cal McKerrol and Pierre Lépine. Ottawa: Information Canada, 1975, 70 pp., paper.

"The purpose of this publication is twofold: to outline human rights legislation . . . and to provide a sampling of pertinent decisions." D

49   Canada. Royal Commission on Bilingualism and Biculturalism. *Report of the Royal Commission on Bilingualism and Biculturalism: Book IV. The Cultural Contribution of the Other Ethnic Groups.* Ottawa: Information Canada, 1970, 352 pp.

Perhaps the best and most comprehensive one-volume examination of ethnicity in Canada. Includes topics such as immigration; ethnicity and economic, political, and social patterns; the retention of language and culture; and cultural contributions in arts and letters. C

50   *Canada and the World.* December 1977. Special Issue: Racism.

Six articles, three on general topics related to prejudice, discrimination, and racism, and three case studies. B

51   *Canadians Can Dance* (motion picture). Directed by John Howe. Montreal: National Film Board, 1966. (16mm and 35mm, 22 min., color)

A folk dance festival at the Canadian National Exhibition.

52   Creighton, Helen, ed. *Bluenose Magic: Popular Beliefs and Superstitions in Nova Scotia.* Toronto: McGraw-Hill Ryerson, 1968, 297 pp., cloth.

The ethnic origin of each item is included. C

53   *Ethnic Kaleidoscope Canada.* Nine issues per year, free.

A newsletter published by Information Services, Employment and Immigration Canada.

54   *Everybody's Prejudiced* (motion picture). Directed by Peter Jones. Montreal: National Film Board, 1961. (16mm, 20 min., black and white)

An exploration of prejudice.

55   *Folklorama Winnipeg* (motion picture). Montreal: National Film Board, 1976. (13 min., color)

An ethnic festival.

56   Fowke, Edith, ed. *Folklore of Canada.* Toronto: McClelland and Stewart, 1977, 349 pp., cloth.

Folklore (e.g. folktales, songs, language, riddles, jokes, and rhymes) from the Native Peoples, Canadiens, Anglo-Canadians, and other ethnic groups. C

57   Green, H. Gordon, ed. *A Heritage of Canadian Handicrafts.* Toronto: McClelland and Stewart, 1967, 222 pp., cloth.

The ten chapters contain general sections on the different handicrafts and the particular ethnic crafts of each province. C

58   Gunn, Angus M. *Inequalities within Canada.* Toronto: Oxford University Press, 1974, 60 pp., paper.

Inequalities due to poverty, sex, ethnicity, and regional disparity are described. B

59   Hill, Daniel G. *Human Rights in Canada: A Focus on Racism.* Ottawa: Canadian Labour Congress, 1977, 44 pp., paper.

A well-written booklet, suitable for school use, emphasizing solutions to the problem. C

60   *Manitoba: Festival Country* (motion picture). Montreal: National Film Board, 1970. (27 min., color)

Ethnic folk arts.

61   *Multiculturalism.* Quarterly.

Designed for educators and other professionals working in the area of multiculturalism.

62   *Multi News.* Occasional, free.

A newsletter from the Multiculturalism Directorate, Department of the Secretary of State.

63   *Northern Mosaic.* Bimonthly.

Published by the Thunder Bay Multicultural Association. Contains articles on general topics as well as articles on many ethnic groups.

64   *Our Street Was Paved with Gold* (motion picture). Directed by Albert Kish. Montreal: National Film Board, 1973. (16mm, 28 min., color)

Ethnic diversity in Montreal's St. Lawrence Boulevard, the heart of the city's "little Europe."

65   "Racism: New Victims of an Old Sickness." *Canada and the World*, April 1977, pp. 6-7. B

66   Richmond, Anthony H. "Toronto's Ethnic Ghettoes." *Canadian Forum*, May 1972, pp. 58-60.

Based on a survey of ethnic residential patterns and attitudes toward ethnic diversity in residential districts. D

67 Stern, Doris, and MacKenzie, Helen. *Slurs, Stereotypes and Prejudice.* Hamilton, Ont.: Hamilton Anti-Racism Committee, n.d., 16 pp., paper.

Useful resource book for the study of prejudice and discrimination. C

68 Stymiest, David H. *Order and Disorder: Ethnic Relations in North West Ontario.* Toronto: Peter Martin Associates, 1974, 98 pp., paper and cloth.

Interethnic relations in a small town. D

69 "Toronto: The Icebox Melteth." *Time,* 10 July 1972, pp. 9-12.

The impact of ethnic diversity on Toronto's character. C

70 *Twenty Million People* (motion picture). Montreal: National Film Board, 1967. (16mm, 25 min., color)

Canada's ethnic diversity is portrayed through music and folk dance.

71 White, Charles A. "Are Canadians Prejudiced?" *Canada and the World,* October 1975, pp. 6-7. B

72 Wolfe, Morris. "Purity: The Struggle for WASP Supremacy." *Saturday Night,* December 1977, p. 26.

Attitudes toward ethnic diversity as reflected in *Saturday Night,* 1887-1945. D

73 Woodsworth, James S. *Strangers within Our Gates: Or Coming Canadians.* 1909. Reprint ed. Introduction by Marilyn Barber. Toronto: University of Toronto Press, 1972, 279 pp., paper and cloth.

Woodsworth describes ethnic groups in Canada in 1909 and comments on the impact of immigration on immigrants and Canadian society as a whole. His attitudes toward specific ethnic groups are revealing because he represents liberal thought of his day. D

IMMIGRATION
(Immigration history, policy, and the immigrant experience)

74 Alberro, Ana Lizon, and Montero, Gloria. "'The Land of Beginning Again.'" *Canadian Forum,* September 1975, pp. 23-28.

A study of the experiences of 100 Latin American women who immigrated to Canada between 1969 and 1973. D

75 Alderman, Tom. "One Phone Call Away from Botota: The Short, Jumpy Life of an Illegal Immigrant." *Canadian,* 20 November 1976, pp. 14-15. B

76 Ashworth, Mary. *Immigrant Children in Canadian Schools.* Toronto: McClelland and Stewart, 1975, 228 pp., paper. D

77 ———. "The Settlement of Immigrants in Greater Vancouver." *Canadian Welfare,* March/April 1977, pp. 9-13.

A study of the services available to immigrants in Vancouver. C

78 Bailey, Leuba, ed. *The Immigrant Experience.* Toronto: Macmillan, 1975, 122 pp., paper.

   A literary anthology. B

79 *The Bias of Culture* (audiotape). Toronto: Canadian Broadcasting Corporation, 1972/73. (90 min., three programs, reel and cassette)

   The problems of immigrants thrust into an alien culture.

80 Blake, Roy. "Saying 'No' to the Alien Hordes." *Saturday Night*, July/August 1976, pp. 32-37.

   A former employee describes the immigration department. C

81 *Blue-Collar Immigrants* (audiotape). Toronto: Canadian Broadcasting Corporation, n.d. (30 min., reel and cassette)

   Five Slavic immigrants are interviewed.

82 Broadfoot, Barry. *The Pioneer Years 1895-1914: Memories of Settlers Who Opened the West.* Toronto: Doubleday, 1976, 384 pp., cloth.

   The stories of Western pioneers, as told to Broadfoot.

83 Bruce, Jean. *The Last Best West.* Don Mills: Fitzhenry and Whiteside, 1976, 192 pp., paper and cloth.

   A pictorial history, accompanied by short essays, of the settlement of the West during the Sifton era. B

84 Canada. Department of Manpower and Immigration. Canadian Immigration and Population Study. *Immigration Policy Perspectives* (77 pp.); *The Immigration Program* (233 pp.); *Immigration and Population Statistics* (126 pp.); *Three Years in Canada: First Report of the Longitudinal Survey on the Economic and Social Adaptation of Immigrants* (152 pp.). Ottawa: Information Canada, 1974, paper.

   These four volumes constitute the Green Paper on immigration policy. D

85 Canada. Department of Manpower and Immigration. Information Service. *Focus on Canadian Immigration.* By George Bonavia. Ottawa: 1977, 170 pp., free.

   Short articles on topics relevant to Canadian immigration today. C

86 *Canada and the World.* December 1976, Special Issue: Immigration.

   Six articles on immigration history and policy, the immigrant experience, and illegal immigrants. B

87 Cox, Ralph. "A Short History of Canadian Immigration." *Canada and the World*, February 1974, pp. 18-19. B

88 Dickenson, Victoria. *Canada's Multicultural Heritage: A Brief History of Immigration.* Ottawa: National Museum of Man, 1975, n.p., free.

   A chronological outline history illustrated with period photographs and paintings. B

89   Edmonds, Alan. "The War Brides, 30 Years Later." *Canadian*, 15 May 1976, pp. 16-20. B

90   Ferguson, Edith. *Immigrants in Canada.* Rev. ed. Toronto: University of Toronto, Faculty of Education, Guidance Centre, 1977, 48 pp., paper.

This booklet, designed for school use, is an excellent introduction to immigration, the immigrant experience, current immigration policy, and the services available to immigrants. B

91   Ferrante, Angela. "The People Who Don't Belong Here." *Maclean's*, 29 November 1976, p. 44b.

Illegal immigrants. B

92   Harney, Robert, and Troper, Harold. *Immigrants: A Portrait of the Urban Experience, 1890-1930.* Toronto: Van Nostrand Reinhold, 1975, 224 pp., paper.

An interesting blend of photographs, primary sources, and short essays. D

93   Hodgetts, A. B., and Burns, J. D. *Decisive Decades: A History of the Twentieth Century for Canadians.* 2d rev. ed. Toronto: Thomas Nelson, 1973, 512 pp., cloth.

Immigration and the history of the West during the Laurier era receive an extensive treatment in this high school history text. C

94   *Immigrants to Power* (audiotape). Toronto: Canadian Broadcasting Corporation, 1971. (60 min., reel and cassette)

A consideration of "the Canadian power structure and how the various immigrant groups to Canada have been assimilated, or not, within the existing hierarchy."

95   *Immigration* (motion picture or videocassette). Toronto: CTV Television, 1975. (16mm or 3/4" videocassette, 50 min., color)

"A close look at immigration and racism in Canada through a probing investigation of the policies and problems of our immigration scene."

96   "Immigration: Rethinking the Ideal National Mosaic." *Time*, 18 November 1974, pp. 6-7. C

97   "Immigration: A Richer Culture, A Slower Growth." *Time*, 17 February 1975, pp. 8-14.

This article reviews the history of Canadian immigration policies, describes present policies, and the policy alternatives outlined in the Green Paper. Interethnic relations is discussed in terms of "nonwhite-white" relations. C

98   *Immigration to Western Canada 1896-1914* (slides). Ottawa: National Film Board and National Museum of Man, n.d. 30 slides (color and black and white) and 1 teacher's booklet. Distributor: Scholar's Choice.

99   "Immigration: Welcome." *Time*, 16 September 1974, p. 13.

Welcome House in Toronto is a project designed to aid immigrants. B

100 Krehm, Gladys. "The Illegals." *Canadian Forum*, October 1976, pp. 5-7.

One illegal immigrant's story. B

101 Lind, Loren. "New Canadianism: Melting the Ethnics in Toronto Schools." *This Magazine*, August 1973, pp. 6-10.

A critical evaluation of programs for immigrant children in Toronto's schools. C

102 Loney, Martin, and Moscovitch, Allen. "The Immigration Green Paper in Black and White." *Canadian Dimension*, March 1975, pp. 4-8.

The Green Paper is criticized and the relationship between capitalism and racism is explored. D

103 Macdonald, Norman. *Canada Immigration and Colonization: 1841-1903*. Toronto: Macmillan, 1966, paper.

One chapter, "The Melting Pot Era: Group Settlements," discusses the group settlements of the Mennonites, Germans, Scandinavians and Icelanders, Jews and Hungarians, and Doukhobors. D

104 Marr, William L. "Post-War Canadian Immigration and the Canadian Economy." *Quarterly of Canadian Studies for the Secondary School*, 1974, pp. 151-64. D

105 Montero, Gloria. *The Immigrants*. Toronto: James Lorimer, 1977, 222 pp., cloth.

The immigrant experience is vividly portrayed by immigrants telling their own stories. B

106 *The Opening of the Canadian West* (kit). Scarborough: Prentice-Hall Media, 1972. 3 filmstrips, 3 cassettes, and 1 teacher's guide.

Surveys western Canadian history from early exploration to the present. Part 2 focusses on the Native Peoples and settlement prior to World War I.

107 Palmer, Howard, ed. *Immigration and the Rise of Multiculturalism*. Toronto: Copp Clark, 1975, 215 pp., paper.

A documentary account of immigration and ethnic groups in Canada from 1867 to the present. There are chapters on immigration policy, economic, social, and political adjustment of immigrants, and ethnic organizations. C

108 *The Promised Land* (motion picture). Directed by Carol Myers. Toronto: Canadian Broadcasting Corporation, 1976. (16mm, 55 min., color). Distributor: National Film Board.

Settlement of the prairies.

109 Richmond, Anthony H. *Post-War Immigrants in Canada*. Toronto: University of Toronto Press, 1967, 320 pp., cloth.

Based on two investigations of post-war immigrants. The first (1961) surveyed a representative sample of post-war immigrants, and the second (1962-63) studied British immigrants who had returned home. E

110 Sanderson, George. "Immigration: A Look at Present Trends." *Labour Gazette*, January 1975, pp. 31-39.

A useful background paper. C

111 Slopen, Beverley, interviewer. "Twenty Years into the Milk and Honey." *Canadian*, 7 August 1976, pp. 4-6.

The success stories of six immigrants. B

112 *The Sometime Samaritan Part II* (motion picture or videocassette). Toronto: CTV Television, 1976. (16mm, or 3/4" videocassette, 25 min., color)

The program examines "the good and bad of Canada's erratic refugee policy by taking viewers into the refugee camps of Europe...." One program in the "Maclear" series.

113 Tait, R. M. "The Canadian Immigration and Population Study." *Alternatives*, vol. 3, no. 3, 1974, pp. 17-18.

The Green Paper on immigration was prepared by this study group. This article describes the origins of the study group, its purposes, and some of the issues it explored as it prepared the Green Paper. D

114 *This Is a Photograph* (motion picture). Directed by Albert Kish. Montreal: National Film Board, 1971. (16mm and 35mm, 10 min., color)

Immigrants' impressions of Canada presented through a collection of photographs.

115 Thomas, David. "How We Keep Out the Black and the Yellow." *Saturday Night*, June 1972, p. 12.

The author argues that there is a strong racist bias in our present immigration policies. C

116 Wolfgang, Aaron, ed. *Education of Immigrant Students: Issues and Answers.* Toronto: Ontario Institute for Studies in Education, 1975, 224 pp., paper.

A collection of papers presented at the National Conference on the Education of Immigrant Students, 1974. D

MULTICULTURALISM AND BILINGUALISM

117 Arnold, A. J. "How Far Do We Go with Multi-culturalism?" *Canadian Ethnic Studies*, vol. 2, no. 2, 1970, pp. 7-14. D

118 *Bons amis* (motion picture). Montreal: National Film Board, 1974. (16mm, 12 min., color)

A look at the Official Languages Act and the role of the Commissioner of Official Languages.

119 Canada. Canadian Consultative Council on Multiculturalism. *First Annual Report of the Canadian Consultative Council on Multiculturalism.* Ottawa: 1975, 53 pp., paper, free.

The CCCM's recommendations to the minister responsible for multiculturalism. C

120 ——. *Multiculturalism as State Policy: Conference Report.* Ottawa: 1976, 200 pp., paper, free.

An important collection of papers from the Second Canadian Conference on Multiculturalism, presenting the reactions of politicians, journalists, and the English- and French-Canadian communities to the policy and programs of multiculturalism. Two chapters describing research studies about attitudes toward multiculturalism and non-official language use and knowledge are included. D

121 Canada. Royal Commission on Bilingualism and Biculturalism. *Bilingualism and Biculturalism: An Abridged Version of the Royal Commission Report.* Edited by Hugh R. Innis. Toronto: McClelland and Stewart, 1973, 186 pp., paper and cloth. D

122 ——. *Report of the Royal Commission on Bilingualism and Biculturalism: Book IV. The Cultural Contribution of the Other Ethnic Groups.* Ottawa: Information Canada, 1970, 352 pp., paper.

Pages 228-30 contain the Commission's recommendations regarding "the measures that should be taken to safeguard the contribution made by the other ethnic groups to the cultural enrichment of Canada." C

123 *Canada: Melting Pot or Mosaic?* (audiotape). Toronto: Canadian Broadcasting Corporation, 1971. (30 min., reel and cassette)

124 "Canada: A Terminal Failure to Communicate?" *Maclean's*, 1 November 1976, p. 18.

The controversy surrounding the federal government's bilingualism policy and programs. C

125 "Canadian Mosaic: Support from Ottawa." *Canada and the World*, February 1972, pp. 6-7.

A description of the federal government's multiculturalism policy and programs announced in November 1971. B

126 Costa, Elio. "Multiculturalism." *Canadian Forum*, November 1971, p. 5.

An editorial. D

127 Creighton, Donald. "Myth of Biculturalism or the Great French-Canadian Sales Campaign." *Saturday Night*, September 1966, pp. 35-39.

Creighton is critical of bilingualism and biculturalism. D

128 Fraser, Graham. "Plains of Abraham, Part Two." *Maclean's*, 18 October 1976, pp. 18-19.

The controversy surrounding the use of French in the air-transport industry. C

129 Gotlieb, Sandra. "A Feast from the Roots: Multiculturalism Is Beautiful." *Maclean's*, December 1973, p. 22.

Toronto's annual Metro International Caravan. B

130 Gwyn, Sandra. "Multiculturalism: A Threat and a Promise." *Saturday Night*, February 1974, pp. 15-18.

An analysis of the multiculturalism policy and programs. C

131 ——. "Speaking the Unspeakable, Bilingually." *Saturday Night*, July/August 1976, p. 10.

A critical review of bilingualism programs in the federal civil service. C

132 Jackson, Robin, comp. "Development of the Multicultural Policy in Canada: A Bibliography." *Canadian Library Journal*, vol. 33, no. 3, 1976, pp. 237-43.

133 MacGuigan, Mark. "Libraries in the Canadian Mosaic: Keynote Address." *Canadian Library Journal*, vol. 33, no. 5, pp. 429-32.

An address delivered by MacGuigan (on behalf of John Munro, then Minister Responsible for Multiculturalism) at the Canadian Library Association's "Libraries in the Canadian Mosaic" conference. C

134 Montero, Gloria. "Facing up to Multiculturalism." *Canadian Forum*, May 1976, pp. 12-13. D

135 Murphy, Rae. "The Unmaking of the Minister of Culture." *Last Post*, September 1973, pp. 27-31.

The politics of multiculturalism while Dr. Stanley Haidasz was Minister of State for Multiculturalism. D

136 *A National Understanding: The Official Languages of Canada.* Ottawa: Supply and Services Canada, 1977, 78 pp., paper.

"Statement of the Government of Canada on the official languages policy." D

137 Osicki, Richard. "The Agony of Julius Koteles." *Weekend Magazine*, 5 March 1977, pp. 14-15.

Koteles was Chairman of the Canadian Consultative Council on Multiculturalism until 1976. This article presents his aspirations and frustrations. C

138 Palmer, Howard. "Canada: Multicultural or Bicultural?" *Canadian Ethnic Studies*, vol. 3, no. 1, 1971, pp. 109-18.

An analysis of the federal government's multiculturalism policy. D

139 Remnant, Robert. "Vive la Différence." *Canada and the World*, October 1976, pp. 12-13.

A concise discussion of the federal government's multiculturalism policy, its origins, multicultural programs, critical response, and the way ahead. B

140 Schecter, Sandra. "Bilingualism Debate: Is There Life after Adolescence?" *Last Post*, December 1976, pp. 6-7.

The controversy, as generated by a report by K. Spicer and a study by G. Bibeau, surrounding the training of federal civil servants to be bilingual. C

141 Torson, J. T. *Wanted: A Single Canada.* Toronto: McClelland and Stewart, 1973, 160 pp., cloth.

A critique of the federal policy of bilingualism. D

142 Troper, Harold. "Multiculturalism: The Heritage Ontario Congress." *Canadian Forum*, September 1972, pp. 2-4. D

143 White, Charles A. "Bilingualism: Backlash Building." *Canada and the World*, April 1976, pp. 6-7.

The controversy surrounding federal language policies and programs and Quebec's Bill 22. B

144 ——. "Bilingualism: Canada's Language Barrier." *Canada and the World*, January 1973, pp. 12-13.

The federal government's bilingualism policy and programs. B

ETHNIC STUDIES (Social science literature and curriculum and instruction)

145 Banks, James A. "Ethnic Studies as a Process of Curriculum Reform." *Social Education*, vol. 40, no. 2, 1976, pp. 76-80.

Throughout his work Banks emphasizes an inquiry-oriented, interdisciplinary, and comparative approach to ethnic studies in school programs. In addition, he stresses that ethnic studies content be included in all school programs, not just in separate courses.

146 ——. "Evaluating the Multi-ethnic Components of the Social Studies." *Social Education*, vol. 40, no. 7, 1976, pp. 538-41.

147 ——. "Teaching Ethnic Studies: Key Issues and Concepts." *Social Studies*, vol. 66, no. 3, 1975, pp. 107-13.

148 ——. "Teaching for Ethnic Literacy: A Comparative Approach." *Social Education*, vol. 37, no. 8, 1973, pp. 738-50.

149 ——. *Teaching Strategies for Ethnic Studies.* Boston: Allyn and Bacon, 1975, 502 pp., paper.

A basic curriculum and instruction text for pre- and in-service teachers.

150 Banks, James A.; Cortés, C. E.; Gay, G.; Garcia, R. L.; and Ochoa, A. S. *Curriculum Guidelines for Multiethnic Education: Position Statement.* Arlington, Va.: National Council for the Social Studies, 1976, 48 pp., paper.

Published as an insert in vol. 40, no. 6 (1976) of *Social Education*. Presents a rationale for ethnic pluralism and guidelines for pluralistic curricula and school environments. This, perhaps, is the best statement of its kind.

151 Berry, Brewton, and Tischler, Henry L. *Race and Ethnic Relations.* 4th ed. Boston: Houghton Mifflin Co., forthcoming, cloth.

An introductory text at the college level.

152 Canada. Department of Manpower and Immigration. Canadian Immigration and Population Study. *Aspects of the Absorption and Adaptation of Immigrants.* By Anthony H. Richmond. Ottawa: Information Canada, 1974, 51 pp., paper.

Important teacher reference material for a study of the immigrant experience.

153 Cortés, Carlos E.; Metcalf, Fay; and Hawke, Sharryl. *Understanding You and Them: Tips for Teaching about Ethnicity.* Boulder, Colo.: ERIC Clearinghouse for Social Studies/Social Science Education, Social Science Education Consortium, 1976, 61 pp., paper.

154 Driedger, Leo, ed. *Canadian Ethnic Mosaic.* Toronto: McClelland and Stewart, 1978, 335 pp., paper.

Proceedings of Canadian Ethnic Studies Association Conference 1975.

155 Elliott, Jean Leonard, ed. *Minority Canadians 1: Native Peoples.* Scarborough, Ont.: Prentice-Hall, 1971, 169 pp., paper.

Chapter 1, "Minority Groups: A Canadian Perspective," provides a concise introduction to the study of ethnic minority groups.

156 *Ethnic Heritage Studies Materials Analysis Instrument.* Boulder, Colo.: Social Science Education Consortium, 1975, 22 pp., paper.

Useful for comparative evaluations of instructional materials.

157 Gordon, Milton Myron. *Assimilation in American Life: The Role of Race, Religion, and National Origins.* New York: Oxford University Press, 1964, 276 pp., cloth.

A highly readable and comprehensive introduction to the field of ethnic studies. Gordon is one of the United States's foremost students of ethnicity.

158 *The History and Social Science Teacher*, vol. 12, no. 1, 1976. Special Issue: Multiculturalism.

Eight articles relevant to curriculum and instruction in ethnic studies.

159 Hughes, David, and Kallen, Evelyn. *The Anatomy of Racism: Canadian Dimensions.* Montreal: Harvest House, 1974, 230 pp., paper and cloth.

Chapters 6-11 provide an excellent introduction to many of the concepts in the field of ethnic studies.

160 *Human Relations.* Annual, free.

Published by the Ontario Human Rights Commission. Each issue contains a variety of articles and perspectives on human rights issues.

161 Isajiw, W. W. "Olga in Wonderland: Ethnicity in Technological Society." *Canadian Ethnic Studies*, vol. 9, no. 1, 1977, pp. 77-85.

Isajiw explores ethnic identification in North American societies. Of particular interest is his discussion of ethnic rediscoverers: people who have been socialized in the majority culture but have sought out and identified with their ethnic background.

162 Isajiw, W. W., ed. *Identities: The Impact of Ethnicity on Canadian Society*. Toronto: Peter Martin Associates, 1977, 221 pp., paper and cloth.

Papers presented to the second biannual Canadian Ethnic Studies Association conference in 1973. In particular, the papers by Jaenen, "Ethnic Studies—An Integral Part of Canadian Studies," Palmer, "History and Present State of Ethnic Studies in Canada," and Breton et al., "The Impact of Ethnic Groups on Canadian Society: Research Issues" provide important insights into the nature of ethnic studies.

163 Kehoe, John. "Multiculturalism and the Problems of Ethical Relativism." *History and Social Science Teacher*, vol. 13, no. 1, 1977, pp. 23-26.

Kehoe argues that the cultural relativism implied in multiculturalism is desirable except in the area of ethical issues. These should not be viewed from the relativist position but should be examined according to a set of ethical principles, which he identifies.

164 Kovacs, M. L., and Cropley, A. J. "Assimilation and Alienation in Ethnic Groups." *Canadian Ethnic Studies*, vol. 4, nos. 1-2, 1972, pp. 13-24.

As ethnic group members are assimilated into the dominant society they become alienated from their own group.

165 McDiarmid, Garnet, and Pratt, David. *Teaching Prejudice: A Content Analysis of Social Studies Textbooks Authorized for Use in Ontario*. Toronto: Ontario Institute for Studies in Education, 1971, 131 pp., paper.

166 Mang, Lesley. *Resources for Multicultural Programs*. Toronto: Learnxs Press, 1976, 60 pp., paper.

A guide for organizing multicultural programs, with primary emphasis on school-based projects.

167 Migus, Paul, ed. *Sounds Canadian: Languages and Culture in Multi-ethnic Society*. Toronto: Peter Martin Associates, 1975, cloth.

Papers presented at the 1971 Canadian Ethnic Studies Association conference.

168 Nakamura, Mark. "The Teacher's Role in the Fight against Discrimination." *History and Social Science Teacher*, vol. 12, no. 2, 1976, pp. 100-102.

169 Palmer, Howard, and Troper, Harold. "Canadian Ethnic Studies: Historical Perspectives and Contemporary Implications." *Interchange*, vol. 4, no. 4, 1973, pp. 15-23.

170 Porter, John. "Canada: Dilemmas and Contradictions of a Multi-Ethnic Society." In *Sociology Canada: Readings*, pp. 3-15. Edited by C. Beattie and S. Crysdale. Toronto: Butterworth, 1974, paper.

171 ———. "Ethnic Pluralism in Canadian Perspective." In *Ethnicity: Theory and Experience*, pp. 267-304. Edited by N. Glazier and D. P. Moynihan. Cambridge: Harvard University Press, 1975, paper and cloth.

172 ———. *The Vertical Mosaic: An Analysis of Social Class and Power in Canada*. Toronto: University of Toronto Press, 1965, 626 pp., paper and cloth.

Chapter 3 discusses the relationship between ethnicity and social class in Canada.

173 Vallee, Frank G. "Multi-ethnic Societies: The Issues of Identity and Inequality." In *Issues in Canadian Society: An Introduction to Sociology*, pp. 162-202. Edited by D. Forcese and S. Richer. Scarborough: Prentice-Hall, 1975, paper and cloth.

An excellent introduction to key social science concepts.

174 Vallee, Frank G.; Schwarz, M.; and Darknell, F. "Ethnic Assimilation and Differentiation in Canada." In *Canadian Society: Sociological Perspectives*. 3d ed. Pp. 593-603. Edited by Bernard R. Blishen et al. Toronto: Macmillan, 1968, cloth.

175 Werner, Walter; Connors, B.; Aoki, T.; and Dahlie, J. *Whose Culture? Whose Heritage?: Ethnicity within Canadian Social Studies Curricula*. Vancouver: University of British Columbia, Faculty of Education, Centre for the Study of Curriculum and Instruction, 1977, 65 pp. Distributor: University Bookstore.

A report based on an examination of social studies curricula in all provinces and territories.

176 Wirth, Louis. "The Problem of Minority Groups." In *Minority Responses: Comparative Views of Reactions to Subordination*, pp. 34-42. Edited by Minako Kurakawa. New York: Random House, 1970.

Wirth explores the concept ethnic minority group and analyses the ways such a group can react to its status.

Ethnic Groups

AMERICANS

177 Christy, Jim, ed. *The New Refugees: American Voices in Canada*. Toronto: Peter Martin, 1972, 151 pp., cloth.

A collection of writings by war resisters. D

178 Friedenberg, Edgar Z. "Americans: Canada's New Jews?" *Axiom*, October/November 1975, pp. 24-27.

A serious look at American immigrants in Canada and Canadian attitudes toward them. In the process Friedenberg comments on the nature of Canadian society. D

179 Fulford, Robert. "Our Newest Minority, the Young American Draft Dodgers...." *Saturday Night*, November 1968, pp. 11-12. C

180 Johnson, Valerie Miner. "American Women in Canada." *Chatelaine*, May 1973, p. 48.

The experiences and views of five immigrants. B

181 Ruddy, Jon. "The Americans Who Voted with Their Feet." *Maclean's*, March 1969, p. 27.

The increased immigration of Americans into Canada in the late 1960s. B

182 ——. "Calgaryanks." *Maclean's*, 3 September 1966, pp. 18-20.

The oil boom in Alberta resulted in an influx of Americans (30 000) into Calgary. C

183 Troper, Harold Martin. *Only Farmers Need Apply: Official Canadian Government Encouragement of Immigration from the United States, 1896-1911.* Toronto: Griffin, 1972, 192 pp., cloth. D

AMISH

184 Fulford, Robert. "Have the Amish a Place in Our Liberal Society?" *Saturday Night*, December 1977, pp. 19-21.

The controversy between the Ontario Milk Marketing Board and the Amish regarding the use of electrically cooled milk storage tanks. The religious precepts of the Amish condemn the use of electricity. C

185 Gingerich, Orland. *The Amish of Canada.* Waterloo: Conrad Press, 1972, 244 pp., cloth.

A history of the Amish in Canada. D

186 Staebler, Edna. *Sauerkraut and Enterprise.* Toronto: McClelland and Stewart, 1969, 96 pp.

This fascinating and highly personal little book gives the reader an excellent introduction to the Old Order Mennonite and Amish cultures. B

BELGIANS

187 Breugelmans, René. "Dutch and Flemings in Canada." *Canadian Ethnic Studies*, vol. 2, no. 2, 1970, pp. 83-115.

The most comprehensive work available. C

188 Wilson, Keith, and Wyndels, James B. *The Belgians in Manitoba.* Winnipeg: Peguis, 1976, 100 pp., paper and cloth.

A history of the Flemings and Walloons in Manitoba. C

BLACKS (See also West Indians)

189 *Bibliography of Centre's Resources on the West Indian/Black Communities in*

Canada and Toronto and Related Materials. Toronto: Cross-Cultural Communication Centre, 7 pp., mimeo, free.

190 *Black Like Me* (audiotape). Toronto: Canadian Broadcasting Corporation, 1969. (60 min.)

Griffin, author of *Black Like Me*, talks of his experiences while living as a Black in United States. He draws parallels between United States and Canada.

191 Blakeley, Phyllis R. "Boston King: A Negro Loyalist Who Sought Refuge in Nova Scotia." *Dalhousie Review*, vol. 48, no. 3, 1968, pp. 347-56. D

192 "Canada's Negroes: An Untold Story." *U.S. News and World Report*, 11 May 1970, pp. 46-48.

A survey of Black communities in Toronto, Windsor, Montreal, and Halifax. C

193 Clairmont, Donald H., and Magill, Dennis William. *Africville: The Life and Death of a Canadian Black Community.* Toronto: McClelland and Stewart, 1974, 272 pp., paper.

The people of Africville, a depressed Black community within the City of Halifax, were relocated during the 1960s. A sociological study. D

194 Cox, Ralph. "The Underground Railroad: Freedom Far from Slavery, and the Role Canada Played." *Canada and the World*, May 1973, pp. 22-23. B

195 Drew, Benjamin. *The Refugee: On the Narratives of Fugitive Slaves in Canada.* 1856. Reprint ed. Rexdale, Ont.: Coles, 1972, 387 pp., paper.

The author interviewed and recorded the life stories of slaves who had escaped to Canada. C

196 *Encounter at Kwacha House–Halifax* (motion picture). Directed by Bonny Klein and Rex Tasker. Montreal: National Film Board, 1967. (16mm, 17 min., black and white)

A discussion among Black and white youths.

197 Erland, Anastasia. "The New Blacks in Canada." *Saturday Night*, January 1970, pp. 17-19.

Toronto's Black community in 1970. C

198 "First Black Power Town." *Ebony*, February 1972, pp. 91-95.

A history of the Black community in Buxton, Ontario. C

199 Foner, Philip S. "The Colored Inhabitants of Vancouver Island." *BC Studies*, no. 8, 1970-71. pp. 29-33.

A reprint of an article, with an introduction by Foner, written in 1864 by a Black about the plight of Blacks in Victoria. D

200 Fraser, Doug. "The Forgotten Canadians." *Canada and the World*, December 1977, pp. 14-15.

The Black community in Nova Scotia. B

201 Grow, Stewart. "The Blacks of Amber Valley: Negro Pioneering in Northern Alberta." *Canadian Ethnic Studies*, vol. 6, nos. 1-2, 1974, pp. 17-38.

Several hundred Blacks left Oklahoma from 1910 to 1912 and settled in Alberta. D

202 Harvey, Evelyn B. "The Negro Loyalists." *Nova Scotia Historical Quarterly*, vol. 1, no. 3, 1971, pp. 181-202. D

203 Henry, Frances. *Forgotten Canadians: The Blacks of Nova Scotia.* Don Mills: Longman, 1973, 215 pp., paper.

A research report based on a study which measured the attitudes and values of Black Nova Scotians. Considerable background material on Nova Scotia's Black communities and two specific settlements is provided. E

204 Henry, Franklin J. *The Experience of Discrimination: A Case Study Approach.* San Francisco: R and E Research Associates, 1974, 104 pp., paper.

A study, conducted in 1964, of discrimination as experienced by the Blacks and Japanese of Hamilton, Ontario. D

205 How, Douglas. "The Holy Town Will Have to Take Its Halo Down." *Weekend Magazine*, 7 October 1972, pp. 3-7.

Black-white relations in Antigonish, Nova Scotia. C

206 "In Search of a Sense of Community." *Time*, 6 April 1970, pp. 8-11.

Canada's Black community in 1970. C

207 Koné, Boubacar. "Being Black in Montreal." *Maclean's*, December 1968, pp. 46-47. C

208 Lubka, Nancy. "Ferment in Nova Scotia." *Queen's Quarterly*, vol. 76, no. 2, 1969, pp. 213-28.

An overview of Black-white relations in 1969. D

209 McIntyre, Paul. *Black Pentecostal Music in Windsor.* Ottawa: National Museum of Man, Canadian Centre for Folk Culture Studies, 1976, 124 pp., paper. D

210 Oliver, Jules. "Games Blacks and Whites Play." *Labour Gazette*, vol. 70, no. 6, 1970, pp. 400-408.

Oliver discusses the psychological dimension of Black-white relations and suggests ways of breaking down racial barriers, especially in education. D

211 Ontario. Ontario Human Rights Commission. *The Black Presence in the Canadian Mosaic: A Study of Perception and the Practise of Discrimination against Blacks in Metropolitan Toronto.* By Wilson A. Head. Toronto, 1975, 235 pp., free. D

212 ———. *A Brief Pictorial History of Blacks in Nineteenth Century Ontario.* Toronto, n.d., n.p., free.

Capsule biographies and pictures of prominent Blacks. A

213 Quig, James. "Walking Black through Halifax." *Weekend Magazine*, 19 June 1976, pp. 4-6.

The barriers of segregation are gradually breaking down. New attitudes and hopes are appearing among both Blacks and whites. C

214 Balston, H. Keith. "John Sullivan Deas: A Black Entrepreneur in British Columbia Salmon Canning." *BC Studies*, no. 32, 1976-77, pp. 64-78.

Deas arrived in British Columbia from the United States in 1862. C

215 Rawlyk, G. A. "The Guysborough Negroes: A Study in Isolation." *Dalhousie Review*, vol. 48, no. 1, 1968, pp. 24-36. D

216 Schweninger, Loren. "A Fugitive Negro in the Promised Land: James Rapier in Canada, 1836-1864." *Ontario History*, vol. 61, no. 2, 1975, pp. 91-104. D

217 Sessing, Trevor W. "How They Kept Canada Almost Lily White." *Saturday Night*, September 1970, pp. 30-32.

Canadian immigration officials stopped American Blacks from entering Canada (1909-1911) because of racial prejudice. C

218 *Seven Shades of Pale* (motion picture). Directed by Les Rose. Montreal: National Film Board, 1975. (16mm, 28 min., color)

An examination of the changes occurring in Black communities in Nova Scotia.

219 Smucker, Barbara. *Underground to Canada.* Toronto: Clarke Irwin, 1977, 157 pp., cloth.

A historical novel about the Underground Railway. B

220 Spray, W. A. *The Blacks in New Brunswick.* Fredericton: Brunswick Press, 1972, 95 pp., paper.

A history. C

221 Tait, Terence D., ed. *Black and White in North America: Selected Sources.* Toronto: McClelland and Stewart, 1970, 83 pp., paper.

A sourcebook for high school use. Focusses on both United States and Canada. C

222 Tulloch, Headley. *Black Canadians: A Long Line of Fighters.* Toronto: NC Press, 1975, 186 pp., paper.

A history. C

223 Walker, James W. St. G. *The Black Loyalists: The Search for a Promised Land in Nova Scotia and Sierra Leone 1783-1870.* New York: Africana Publishing. Halifax: Dalhousie University Press, 1976, 438 pp., paper and cloth. D

224 Winks, Robin W. *The Blacks in Canada: A History.* Montreal: McGill-Queen's University Press, 1971, 546 pp., cloth.

A comprehensive scholarly work. D

225 ——. "Negroes in the Maritimes: An Introductory Survey." *Dalhousie Review*, vol. 48, no. 4, 1968-69, pp. 453-71.

A history. D

226 ——. "Negro School Segregation in Ontario and Nova Scotia." *Canadian Historical Review*, vol. 50, no. 2, 1969, pp. 164-91. D

BRITISH (See also English, Irish, Scots, and Welsh)

227 *British Immigration to British North America* (slides). Ottawa: National Film Board and National Museum of Man, n.d. 30 slides (color and black and white) and 1 teacher's booklet. Distributor: Scholar's Choice.

228 Britt, Kent. "The Loyalists." *National Geographic*, April 1975, pp. 510-21. B

229 Charney, A. "What It Means to Be English in a Very French Quebec." *Maclean's*, June 1972, p. 19. C

230 Cowan, Helen I. *British Immigration before Confederation.* Ottawa: Canadian Historical Association, 1968, 24 pp., paper. C

231 Ferrante, Angela, and Dewar, Elaine. "Quebec's English: A Vanishing Minority." *Maclean's*, 4 April 1977, pp. 18-22. C

232 Guillet, Edwin C. *The Great Migration: The Atlantic Crossing by Sailing-ship since 1770.* Toronto: University of Toronto Press, 1963, 301 pp., paper.

The story of eleven million British immigrants who travelled to North America between 1770 and 1890. D

233 *Loyalist Country* (motion picture). Montreal: National Film Board, 1974. (13 min., color)

The history of and imprint left by the Loyalists of the Richelieu Valley of Quebec.

234 MacDonald, D. "What It's Like to Be English in Montreal." *Chatelaine*, January 1974, p. 33. C

235 Mika, Nick, and Mika, Helma. *United Empire Loyalists: Pioneers of Upper Canada.* Belleville, Ont.: Mika Publishing, 1976, 256 pp., cloth.

A history of the Loyalists in Upper Canada. Their background in the United States is also included. Superbly illustrated. B

236 Morgan, Robert J. "The Loyalists of Cape Breton." *Dalhousie Review*, vol. 55, no. 1, Spring 1975, pp. 5-22.

A detailed history to 1820. D

237 Muggeridge, John. "Why Those Brits Act Like Brits." *Saturday Night*, April 1971, pp. 32-34.

An English immigrant reflects on his thirteen years in Canada, revealing a perspective different from that of immigrants from most other countries. C

238 Osicki, Richard. "Flight from Quebec." *Weekend Magazine*, 25 June 1977, pp. 4-7.

The exodus of English Canadians from Quebec. C

239 *Passage West: Program I–A Dream of Freedom; Program II–The Awakening* (motion picture). Montreal: National Film Board and British Broadcasting Corporation, 1975. (16mm, 52 min. and 53 min., color)

The migration of people from the British Isles and their early experiences in North America during the nineteenth century.

240 *Peace, Order and Prosperity* (motion picture). Directed by Carol Myers. Toronto: Canadian Broadcasting Corporation, 1976. (16mm, 57 min., color) Distributor: National Film Board.

A history of British settlement in Upper Canada.

241 Upton, L. F. S., ed. *The United Empire Loyalists: Men and Myths.* Toronto: Copp Clark, 1967, 174 pp., paper.

A book of readings composed of primary and secondary sources. D

CHILEANS

242 *Steel Blues* (motion picture). Directed by Jorge Fajardo. Montreal: National Film Board, 1976. (16mm, 34 min., color)

The story of a refugee in Montreal coping with his new environment and changed circumstances.

CHINESE (See also Orientals)

243 Baureiss, Gunther. "The Chinese Community in Calgary." *Alberta Historical Review*, vol. 22, no. 2, 1974, pp. 1-8.

A historical study. C

244 ———. "The Chinese Community of Calgary." *Canadian Ethnic Studies*, vol. 3, no. 1, 1971, pp. 43-56.

A sociological study. D

245 Berton, Pierre. *The Last Spike: The Great Railway 1881-1885.* Toronto: McClelland and Stewart, 1971, 478 pp., cloth.

Berton describes (pp. 194-205) the role played by the Chinese in the construction of the C.P.R. D

246 Dawson, J. Brian. "The Chinese Experience in Frontier Calgary: 1885-1910." In *Frontier Calgary: Town, City, and Region 1875-1914.* Edited by Anthony W.

Rasporich and Henry C. Klassen. Calgary: McClelland and Stewart West, 1975, pp. 124-140, paper. D

247 Hardwick, Francis C., ed. *East Meets West: The Chinese in Canada.* Vancouver: Tantalus Research, 1975, 90 pp., paper.

A history, concentrating on the late 1800s and early 1900s. Extensive use of extracts from primary sources. Designed for classroom use. B

248 Hoe, Ban Seng. *Structural Changes of Two Chinese Communities in Alberta, Canada.* Ottawa: National Museum of Man, Canadian Centre for Folk Culture, 1976, 385 pp., paper, free.

This book is based on the author's doctoral dissertation; however, it is relatively free of sociological jargon. D

249 Lai, Chuen-yan. "Chinese Attempts to Discourage Emigration to Canada: Some Findings from the Chinese Archives in Victoria." *BC Studies*, no. 18, 1973, pp. 33-49. D

250 ———. "Chinese Consolidated Benevolent Association in Victoria: Its Origin and Functions." *BC Studies*, no. 15, 1972, pp. 53-67. D

251 ———. "Home Country and Clan Origins of Overseas Chinese in Canada in the Early 1880s." *BC Studies*, no. 27, 1975, pp. 3-29; correction no. 28, 1975-76, p. 100. D

252 Mah, Jay-Dell. "Struggle for Recognition." *Canada and the World*, October 1976, pp. 16-17.

A history of the Chinese in Canada. B

253 Miller, Robert. "Unhyphenated Canadians: A Century Later, the Chinese Have Truly Arrived." *Maclean's*, 18 April 1977, p. 42b.

A history of Chinese Canadians and a description of some aspects of the contemporary Chinese-Canadian community. C

254 Moon, Mary. "Chinatown in Vancouver—Where the West Meets the East in the West." *BC Motorist*, September/October 1973, pp. 14-19.

A description of Vancouver's Chinatown stressing the unusual and exotic. B

255 Morton, James. *In the Sea of Sterile Mountains: The Chinese in British Columbia.* Vancouver: J. J. Douglas, 1974, 280 pp., paper and cloth.

A comprehensive history. D

256 Munro, John A. "British Columbia and the 'Chinese Evil': Canada's First Anti-Asiatic Immigration Law." *Journal of Canadian Studies*, vol. 6, no. 4, 1971, pp. 42-51. D

257 *My Name Is Susan Yee* (motion picture). Montreal: National Film Board. (16mm, 12 min., color)

Urban renewal as it affects Montreal's Chinatown.

258   Ontario. Ministry of Culture and Recreation. Multicultural Development Branch. *Papers on the Chinese Community.* Toronto: n.d., 50 pp., free.

Five papers on social and cultural topics presented at a seminar in Toronto, 1974. C

259   Paupst, K. "A Note on Anti-Chinese Sentiment in Toronto before the First World War." *Canadian Ethnic Studies*, vol. 9, no. 1, 1977, pp. 54-59. D

260   *Quo Vadis, Mrs. Lumb?* (motion picture). Directed by Ron Kelly. Montreal: National Film Board, 1965. (16mm, 27 min., black and white)

The story of a Chinese-Canadian businesswoman.

261   Ross, Val. "Can the Canadian Elite Tolerate the Chinese Invasion?" *Saturday Night*, June 1977, pp. 11-14.

The economic, educational, and professional success of Chinese Canadians, which is creating a new elite. C

262   Roy, Patricia E. "The Preservation of the Peace in Vancouver: The Aftermath of the Anti-Chinese Riot of 1887." *BC Studies*, no. 31, 1976, pp. 44-59. D

263   Sedgwick, C. P., and Willmott, W. E. "External Influences and Emerging Identity: The Evolution of Community Structure among Chinese Canadians." *Canadian Forum*, September 1974, pp. 8-12.

Voluntary associations among Chinese Canadians in the context of their history in Canada. D

264   Stollery, Peter. "The Emergence of the Chinese Establishment." *Toronto Life*, December 1976, pp. 27-35.

The economic elite of Toronto's Chinese community. C

265   Voisey, Paul L. "Two Chinese Communities in Alberta: An Historical Perspective." *Canadian Ethnic Studies*, vol. 2, no. 2, 1970, pp. 15-30. C

266   Willmott, W. E. "Approaches to the Study of the Chinese in British Columbia." *BC Studies*, no. 4, 1970, pp. 38-52.

Surveys British Columbia's Chinese community and suggests areas of research. D

267   ——. "Some Aspects of Chinese Communities in British Columbia Towns." *BC Studies*, no. 1, 1968-69, pp. 27-36.

An examination of the nature of small Chinese communities in smaller British Columbia centres. D

CROATS

268   Bradica, Stjepan. "A Croatian Immigrant on the Frontier." Introduction by Anthony W. Rasporich. *Canadian Ethnic Studies*, vol. 8, no. 2, 1976, pp. 95-102.

An extract from Bradica's memoirs. He describes his first weeks in Canada. C

269 Paveskovic, Nedo. "Croatians in Canada." In *Croatia: Land, People and Culture.* Vol. 2, pp. 479-506. Edited by F. H. Eterovich and C. Spelatin. Toronto: University of Toronto Press, 1970, cloth. D

CZECHS

270 Gellner, John, and Smerek, John. *The Czechs and Slovaks in Canada.* Toronto: University of Toronto Press, 1968, 172 pp., cloth.

Emphasizes European background, settlement in Canada, distinctive organizations, and present-day involvement in Canadian society. D

271 Hicks, Wessely. "Toronto's Czechs: How They've Settled In." *Toronto Life*, March 1969, pp. 42-45.

The Czech refugees who fled their homeland in 1968. C

DANES (See also Scandinavians)

272 Dahlie, Jorgen. "Scandinavian Experiences on the Prairies, 1890-1920: The Frederiksens of Nakomis." In *The Settlement of the West*, pp. 102-113. Edited by Howard Palmer. Calgary: Comprint Publishing, 1977, paper.

A case study of a Danish immigrant family in Saskatchewan in the 1910s and 1920s. D

273 Paulsen, Frank M. *Danish Settlements on the Prairies: Folk Traditions, Immigrant Experiences, and Local History.* Ottawa: National Museum of Man, Canadian Centre for Folk Culture Studies, 1974, 114 pp., paper. C

DOUKHOBORS

274 Betke, Carl. "The Mounted Police and the Doukhobors in Saskatchewan, 1899-1909." *Saskatchewan History*, vol. 27, no. 1, 1974, pp. 1-14. D

275 Cameron, Silver Donald. "Children of Protest." *Weekend Magazine*, 13 November 1976, pp. 16-20.

A follow-up story on the 104 children of the Sons of Freedom Doukhobors who were seized by the British Columbia government in 1953 and made wards of the province. Their parents had refused to send them to school. C

276 *Cultures Do Die: The Doukhobors* (audiotape). Toronto: Canadian Broadcasting Corporation, n.d. (60 min.)

A historical documentary.

277 Davis, Michael Byron. "Freedom of Religion." *Canada and the World*, October 1976, pp. 20-21.

A history of the Doukhobors in Europe and Canada. B

278 Goa, David J. "Doukhobors." *Canadian Collector*, January/February 1976, pp. 87-89.

A brief introduction to Doukhobor history and culture. C

279 Lyons, John. "The (Almost) Quiet Evolution: Doukhobor Schooling in Saskatchewan." *Canadian Ethnic Studies*, vol. 8, no. 1, 1976, pp. 23-37. D

280 Mealing, F. M. *Doukhobor Life: A Survey of Doukhobor Religion, History and Folklore*. Castlegar, B.C.: Kootenay Doukhobor Historical Society and Continneh Books, 1975, 67 pp., paper. C

281 *Mir: A Doukhobor Youth Publication*. Bimonthly.

Features articles on Doukhobor history, organizations, and cultural activities.

282 Popoff, Eli. *Tanya*. Grand Forks, B.C.: Mir Publication Society, 1975, 276 pp., paper and cloth.

A "biography," based on fiction and history, of a Doukhobor woman. The history of the Doukhobors is presented in an interesting manner because of the author's approach. C

283 Popoff, Lloyd, and Popoff, Jim. "Enduring Philosophy." *Beautiful British Columbia*, Summer 1974, pp. 2-10.

A short article, lavishly illustrated, about Doukhobor history and cultural preservation projects in the Kootenay district of British Columbia. B

284 Tarasoff, Koozma J. "Doukhobors—Their Migration Experience." *Canadian Ethnic Studies*, vol. 4, nos. 1-2, 1972, pp. 1-11.

A short history of Doukhobor migrations in Europe and Canada. D

285 Union of Spiritual Communities of Christ. *The Doukhobors in Canada*. Grand Forks: Mir Publications, 1974, n.p., paper.

A brochure including a short essay and many photographs. B

286 Woodcock, George, and Avakanovic, Ivan. *The Doukhobors*. Toronto: McClelland and Stewart, 1977, 382 pp., paper.

A history of the Doukhobors spanning the time from their origin in the eighteenth century to the 1960s in Canada. D

DUTCH

287 Breugelmans, René. "Dutch and Flemings in Canada." *Canadian Ethnic Studies*, vol. 2, no. 2, 1970, pp. 83-116.

The most comprehensive work available. D

288 de Gelder, Willem. *A Dutch Homesteader on the Prairies: The Letters of Willem de Gelder 1910-1913*. Translation and introduction by Herman Ganzevoort. Toronto: University of Toronto Press, 1973, 92 pp., paper and cloth.

De Gelder's letters provide a graphic insight into the experiences of an immigrant homesteader. C

EAST INDIANS (See also South Asians)

289   Ames, Michael M., and Inglis, Joy. "Conflict and Change in B.C. Sikh Family Life." *BC Studies*, no. 20, Winter 1973/74, pp. 15-49.

An excellent paper based on research findings; however, the terminology is very complex. E

290   *Bibliography of Centre's Resources on the East Indian Community in Canada, Toronto and Related Materials.* Toronto: Cross-Cultural Communication Centre, 1977, 5 pp., mimeo, free.

291   *The Canadian India Times.* Semimonthly.

Each issue contains articles about India and Canada's Indian community.

292   De Santana, Hubert. "Score One for the Racists: This Family Is Going Home." *Maclean's*, 7 February 1977, p. 19. B

293   Ferguson, Ted. *White Man's Country: An Exercise in Canadian Prejudice.* Toronto: Doubleday, 1975, 216 pp., cloth.

The *Komagata Maru* incident of 1914. C

294   Ferrante, Angela. "Racism? You Can't Argue with the Facts." *Maclean's*, 7 February 1977, p. 18.

Prejudice and discrimination against East Indians across Canada. B

295   Lower, J. Arthur. "'Official' Racism." *Canada and the World*, December 1977, pp. 16-17.

A history of Orientals and East Indians in British Columbia. B

296   McClellan, Don. "Terror in Toronto." *Toronto Life*, January 1977, p. 37.

Prejudice and discrimination against East Indians in Toronto. C

297   Ontario. Ministry of Culture and Recreation. Multicultural Development Branch. *Papers on the East Indian Community.* Toronto, n.d., 34 pp., paper, free.

Papers providing background information about India and an excellent introduction to the culture of East Indians in Canada. C

298   Sagi, Douglas. "Trying to Take Us at Our Word." *Canadian Magazine*, 8 March 1975, pp. 2-3.

Prejudice and discrimination against East Indians in Vancouver. B

ENGLISH (See also British)

299   Tyrwhitt, Janice. "What Canada Does to the English (and Vice Versa)." *Maclean's*, 2 January 1965, p. 14.

The experiences of postwar English immigrants. C

FINNS (See also Scandinavians)

300 *A Chronicle of Finnish Settlements in Rural Thunder Bay: Bay Street Project No. 2.* Thunder Bay: Thunder Bay Finnish-Canadian Historical Society, 1976, 151 pp., paper.

Local histories. C

301 *Lakehead University Review,* vol. 9, no. 1, 1976. Special Issue: The Finnish Experience.

Papers presented at a conference at Lakehead University, 1975. D

302 Wilson, J. Donald. "Matti Kurikka: Finnish-Canadian Intellectual." *BC Studies*, no. 20, Winter 1973/74, pp. 50-65.

A biography of M. Kurikka, emphasizing his role in a Finnish utopian socialist community on Malcolm Island, British Columbia. D

FRENCH

303 *Acadia, Acadia* (motion picture). Directed by Michel Brault and Pierre Perrault. Montreal: National Film Board, 1971. (16mm, 75 min., black and white)

A documentary portraying Acadian youth struggling for greater recognition of the French fact in New Brunswick and searching for a clearer understanding of their own identity.

304 Albinski, Henry S. "Quebec and Canadian Unity." *Current History*, vol. 56, no. 392, 1974, pp. 155-60.

Good background essay. D

305 Belliveau, J. E. "The Acadian French and Their Language." *Canadian Geographical Journal*, October/November 1977, pp. 46-55. C

306 Bergeron, Leandre. *The History of Quebec: A Patriote's Handbook.* 2d ed. Toronto: NC Press, 1975, 245 pp., paper.

A Marxist interpretation of Quebec's history. D

307 "Bill 22: Fears, Phantoms and the Law." *Time*, 13 October 1975, pp. 6-7. C

308 Bonenfant, Jean. *The French Canadians and the Birth of Confederation.* 2d ed. Ottawa: Canadian Historical Association, 1970, 22 pp., paper. C

309 Brunet, Michel. *French Canada and the Early Decades of British Rule 1760-1791.* 4th ed. Ottawa: Canadian Historical Association, 1971, 20 pp., paper. C

310 Butler, Rick. "Parlez-Vous Français? You Know It, Boy!" *Maclean's*, September 1975, p. 10.

The French community on the west coast of Newfoundland. C

311 *Canada and the World.* "Separatism," January 1977.

A regular column on topics related to Quebec separatism. B

312 Carlyle-Gordge, Peter. "Endangered Species: Has History Caught Up with Franco-Manitoba?" *Maclean's*, 18 April 1977, p. 44. C

313 Clark, Robert J.; Remnant, R.; Patton, J.; Goulson, C.; and Fors, E. *Canadian Issues and Alternatives.* Toronto: Macmillan, 1974, 241 pp., cloth.

Unit 2 (pp. 58-121) of this text focusses on the question: "How should we cope with the question that has faced generations of Canadians: Quebec in Canada, or Quebec and Canada?" C

314 Creighton, Donald. "No More Concessions." *Maclean's*, 27 June 1977, pp. 24-27.

Creighton argues that English Canada must end its attempts to conciliate Québécois nationalists. C

315 Desbarats, Peter. *René: A Canadian in Search of a Country.* Toronto: McClelland and Stewart, 1976, paper and cloth.

A biography of René Lévesque. D

316 Dreifields, Juris. "Why Quebec Should Not Separate." *Canada and the World*, April 1972, pp. 16-17. B

317 Foulché-Delbose, Isabel. "Women of Three Rivers: 1651-63." In *The Neglected Majority: Essays in Canadian Women's History*, pp. 14-26. Edited by Susan Mann Trofimenkoff and Alison Prentice. Toronto: McClelland and Stewart, 1977, paper. D

318 Fregault, Guy. *Canadian Society in the French Regime.* 7th ed. Ottawa: Canadian Historical Association, 1971, paper. C

319 *The French* (motion picture or videocassette). Toronto: CTV Television, n.d. (16mm, or 3/4" videocassette, 50 min., color)

A history of French Canadians and their struggle for cultural survival.

320 *French-Speaking Settlers on the Prairies 1870-1920* (slides). Ottawa: National Film Board and National Museum of Man, n.d. 30 slides (color and black and white) and 1 teacher's booklet. Distributor: Scholar's Choice.

321 "Future of the French Fact: Four Influential Voices in Quebec 1968 . . ." *Saturday Night*, April 1968, pp. 29-34.

A discussion among C. Ryan, J. Y. Morin, R. Ares, and Y. Groulx. C

322 Glazier, Kenneth M. "Separatism and Quebec." *Current History*, vol. 72, no. 426, 1977, pp. 154-57, 178-79. D

323 Gleason, Marie. "French Immersion: Newfoundland's Outport Experiment." *Axiom*, November/December 1976, pp. 40-41. C

324 Gold, G. L., and Tremblay, M. A., eds. *Communities and Culture in French Canada.* Toronto: Holt, Rinehart and Winston, 1973, 364 pp., paper.

A collection of scholarly papers. E

325 Griffiths, Naomi. *The Acadians: Creation of a People.* Toronto: McGraw-Hill Ryerson, 1973, 94 pp., paper.

A comprehensive introduction to the history of the Acadians focussing on the years 1604 to 1867. A brief chapter examines Acadian nationalism today. D

326 Hodgins, Bruce W.; Bowles, R. P.; Hanley, J. L.; and Rawlyk, G. A. *Canadiens, Canadians and Québécois.* Scarborough, Ont.: Prentice-Hall, 1974, 209 pp., paper.

A book of readings containing sections on the following themes: contemporary and historical English-French relations, policy alternatives for the future, and the contemporary scene in Quebec. C

327 Holbrook, Sabra. *The French Founders of North America and Their Heritage.* New York: Atheneum, 1976, 256 pp., cloth.

Examines the impact of the French on North America in general and on Canada in particular. C

328 Jackson, John D. *Community and Conflict: A Study of French-English Relations in Ontario.* Toronto: Holt, Rinehart and Winston, 1975, 181 pp., paper.

Based on a sociological study conducted in Tecumseh, Ontario. D

329 Jaenen, Cornelius J. *Glimpses of the Franco-Manitoban Community.* Winnipeg: University of Winnipeg Press, 1976, 42 pp., paper.

A history from 1870 to the 1920s. D

330 Johnson, Valerie Miner. "Can French Canada Survive Outside Quebec?" *Saturday Night*, November 1972, pp. 27-29.

An important article focussing on French communities outside of Quebec, emphasizing assimilation and the problems inherent in preventing a complete loss of language and culture. C

331 Joy, Richard J. *Languages in Conflict: The Canadian Experience.* Toronto: McClelland and Stewart, 1972, 149 pp., paper.

A study, based on 1961 census data, of language assimilation among French-speaking Canadians. D

332 Kirbyson, Ronald C. *In Search of Canada.* 2 vols. Scarborough: Prentice-Hall, 1977, 398 pp., and 548 pp., cloth.

An excellent text, useful in this context for the study of French Canada and the history of English-French relations. C

333 *La Nation Québécoise* (audiotape). Toronto: Canadian Broadcasting Corporation, 1971. (60 min., reel and cassette)

"The historical roots and present goals of the French-Canadian nation."

334 *The Language of Modern Québec* (audiotape). Toronto: Canadian Broadcasting Corporation, 1971. (30 min., reel and cassette)

An examination of the French language as spoken in Québec.

335 *La Québécoise* (motion picture). Directed by Les Nirenberg. Montreal: National Film Board, 1972. (16mm, 27 min., color)

The changing status and role of Québécois women.

336 LeBlanc, A. "Bill 22 and the Future of Quebec." *Canadian Forum*, November 1974, pp. 9-10. D

337 LeBlanc, Robert G. "The Acadian Migrations." *Canadian Geographical Journal*, July 1970, pp. 10-19.

A history of the Acadian migrations from the expulsion to the beginning of the 1800s. D

338 Lévesque, René. "Why Quebec Should Separate." *Canada and the World*, April 1972, pp. 18-19. B

339 Levin, Malcolm, and Sylvester, Christine. *Crisis in Quebec.* Toronto: Ontario Institute for Studies in Education, 1973, 102 pp., paper.

The FLQ crisis of 1970. C

340 *Maclean's*, "The Referendum Debate." 2 May 1977.

A regular feature presenting viewpoints on separatism, the national unity debate, and contemporary Quebec. C and D

341 McRoberts, Kenneth. "Bill 22 and Language Policy in Canada." *Queen's Quarterly*, vol. 83, no. 3, 1976, pp. 464-77.

A thorough analysis of Bill 22, language policy in Quebec in general, and the federal bilingualism policy. D

342 *The Magic Circle* (motion picture). Directed by Carol Myers. Toronto: Canadian Broadcasting Corporation, 1976. (16mm, 57 min., color) Distributor: National Film Board.

A history of French Canada from earliest beginnings to 1867.

343 Mallory, J. R. "French and English in Canada: Uneasy Union." *Current History*, vol. 62, no. 368, 1972, pp. 189-93, 210-12.

Important background essay. D

344 Maxwell, Thomas R. *The Invisible French: The French in Metropolitan Toronto.* Waterloo: Wilfrid Laurier University Press, 1977, 174 pp., paper and cloth.

A sociological study. E

345 Miner, Horace. *Saint Denis: A French-Canadian Parish.* Chicago: University of Chicago Press, 1963, paper and cloth.

A sociological study of a rural Quebec parish in the 1930s. D

346 Newman, Christina. "Ottawa Letter: Our Capital? Not for Quebeckers." *Saturday Night*, December 1967, pp. 17-18. C

347 Newman, Peter C. "Question: What Does Quebec Want to Be?" *Maclean's*, May 1971, p. 27.

Ryan's article, no. 356, answers the questions posed in this article. C

348 Nichols, Mark. "Québec: A Report on the State of a Nation." *Maclean's*, 6 September 1976, p. 26.

An in-depth report on Quebec on the eve of the Parti Québécois victory. C

349 Nish, Cameron, ed. *The French Canadians 1759-1766: Conquered? Half-Conquered? Liberated?* Toronto: Copp Clark, 1966, 148 pp., paper.

A book of readings composed of primary and secondary sources. D

350 Popowych, I., and Turcot, P. "Bill 22: The Spectre That Haunts Business in Quebec." *Business Quarterly*, Summer 1975, pp. 59-64. D

351 Posgate, Dale, and McRoberts, Kenneth. *Quebec: Social Change and Political Crisis.* Toronto: McClelland and Stewart, 1976, 216 pp., paper.

An in-depth analysis of Québécois society, politics, economics, and nationalism since the 1950s. D

352 Rioux, Marcel. *Quebec in Question.* Toronto: James Lorimer, 1971, 191 pp., paper and cloth.

"In this book I look at some aspects of Quebec's culture and society. . . . Elsewhere, I speak as a Quebecker who desires the independence of his country." D

353 Rioux, Marcel, and Martin, Ives, eds. *French-Canadian Society.* Vol. 1. Toronto: McClelland and Stewart, 1964, paper.

A collection of scholarly papers. E

354 Rocher, Guy. "The Québec Society: Enigmas to Be Solved." *Forces*, Numéro 34-35, 1er et 2e Trimestres 1976, pp. 98-101.

Perhaps the best examination of contemporary Quebec culture and society. D

355 Rogers, B. S. "Quebec Status . . . The Spoiled Child?" *Canada and the World*, October 1975, pp. 20-21. B

356 Ryan, Claude. "Answer: Quebec Wants to Be Part of a Canada That Recognizes the Needs and Spirit of Not One but Two Nations." *Maclean's*, May 1971, p. 30.

Ryan answers the questions posed by Newman in his article, no. 347. D

357 ———. "The Enigma of French Canada." *Saturday Night*, January 1967, pp. 21-24. D

358 Saywell, John. *The Rise of the Parti Québécois.* Toronto: University of Toronto Press, 1977, 174 pp., paper and cloth. D

359 Simeon, Richard. "The Perils and Politics of Separation." *Maclean's*, October 1971, pp. 23-25. C

360 Skene, Wayne. "Winds of Assimilation: It's Too Late to Save French in St. Boniface." *Weekend Magazine*, 22 May 1976, pp. 20-23. C

361 Stewart, Walter. "My Farewell to Québec." *Maclean's*, June 1975, pp. 27-31.

Stewart has decided that Quebec will eventually separate; so he decided to bid farewell to Quebec with a sense of relief. C

362 Stratford, Philip, and Thomas, Michael. *Voices from Quebec: An Anthology of Translations*. Scarborough: Van Nostrand Reinhold, 1977, 215 pp., paper and cloth.

A literary perspective on Quebec. D

363 *A Sun like Nowhere Else* (motion picture). Directed by Leonard Forest. Montreal: National Film Board, 1972. (16mm, 47 min., color)

Acadians speak of themselves, their concerns, and their hopes for the future.

364 Trueman, Stuart. "The Amazing Comeback." *Atlantic Advocate*, October 1970, p. 28.

A history of the Acadians with an emphasis on the revitalization taking place among the New Brunswick Acadians today. C

365 Urquhart, Ian. "The 'Association' Fallacy." *Maclean's*, 27 June 1977, pp. 28-30.

A critical examination of Lévesque's concept of economic association. C

366 Wade, Mason. *The French Canadians*. Vol. 1, 1760-1911. Rev. ed., 1975. Vol. 2, 1911-1967. Rev. ed., 1967. Toronto: Macmillan, paper.

The foremost historical study. E

367 *Wake Up, mes bons amis* (motion picture). Directed by Pierre Perrault. Montreal: National Film Board, 1970. (16mm, 117 min., black and white)

The nature of nationalism and patriotism.

368 *We Are All . . . Picasso!* (motion picture). Directed by Jacques Giraldeau. Montreal: National Film Board, 1969. (16mm, 58 min., color)

Contemporary Québécois art.

369 White, C. A. "History of Quebec Separatism 1760 to 1972." *Canada and the World*, April 1972, pp. 20-22. B

GERMANS

370 Becker, A. "St. Joseph's Colony, Balgonie." *Saskatchewan History*, vol. 20, no. 1, 1967, pp. 1-18.

The early history of the St. Joseph's community. D

371 Craske, Peter. "Oktoberfest in the German Tradition." *Canadian Review*, October 1976, pp. 39-40. B

372 Fingard, Judith. "How 'Foreign Protestants' Came to Nova Scotia." *Canadian Geographical Journal*, December 1976/January 1977, pp. 54-59.

The majority of the "foreign Protestants" were Germans, who settled in Nova Scotia in the 1750s. D

373 Froeschle, Harmut, ed. *German-Canadian Yearbook*. 3 vols. Toronto: Historical Society of Mecklenburg Upper Canada 1973, 1975, 1976, 347 pp., 293 pp., 304 pp., cloth.

Each volume contains articles on a wide range of topics—for example, multiculturalism, immigration, cultural contribution, immigrant experience, and important individuals. D

374 *Germany* (motion picture or videocassette). Toronto: CTV Television, n.d. (16mm or 3/4" videocassette, 50 min., color)

"Modern Germany and the impact of the German immigrant in Canada."

375 Knight, Phyllis, and Knight, Rolf. *A Very Ordinary Life*. Vancouver: New Star Books, 1974, 317 pp., paper and cloth.

The life story of Phyllis Knight, who immigrated to Canada in 1929. C

376 Kroeker, Wally. "Ethnic Germans Provided Settlement Impetus." *Manitoba Business Journal*, December/January 1969-70, pp. 154-55, 241-43.

A history and description of Manitoba's German community. C

377 Reaman, G. Elmore. *The Trail of the Black Walnut*. Toronto: McClelland and Stewart, 1974, 256 pp., paper.

Reaman documents the immigration of Pennsylvania Germans and related groups to present-day Ontario in the 1700s and early 1800s. D

378 Wagner, Jonathan. "The *Deutscher Bund Canada* 1934-39." *Canadian Historical Review*, vol. 58, no. 2, 1977, pp. 176-200.

"During its six-year existence . . ." the *Bund* "conducted an elaborate propaganda campaign designed to convert Canada's Germans to the 'truths' of National Socialism." D

379 ———. "'Heim Ins Reich,' the Story of Loon River's Nazis." *Saskatchewan History*, vol. 29, no. 2, 1976, pp. 41-50.

Twenty German families homesteaded (1929-1939) in Loon River, Saskatchewan. They became involved in the "Deutscher Bund Canada" and left, in frustration, for Germany in 1939. D

380 White, Charles A. "Oktoberfest and More." *Canada and the World*, October 1976, pp. 18-19.

The history and contributions of German Canadians. B

GREEKS

381 *The 80 Goes to Sparta* (motion picture). Directed by Bill Davies. Montreal: National Film Board, 1969. (16mm, 45 min., black and white)

The Greek community in Montreal.

382 Patterson, G. James. *The Greeks of Vancouver: A Study in the Preservation of Ethnicity.* Ottawa: National Museum of Man, Canadian Centre for Folk Culture Studies, 1976, 162 pp., paper. C

383 Persons, Heather. "Vancouver's Greek Community." *BC Motorist*, November/December 1973, pp. 44-47.

A journalistic examination of the culture of the Greek community. C

HUNGARIANS

384 *Bekevar Jubilee* (motion picture). Directed by Albert Kish. Montreal: National Film Board, 1977. (16mm, 27 min., color)

The story of the Bekevar community in Saskatchewan and its celebrations marking its 75th anniversary.

385 Degh, Linda. *People in the Tobacco Belt: Four Lives.* Ottawa: National Museum of Man, Canadian Centre for Folk Culture Studies, 1975, 277 pp., paper.

The life histories of four Hungarian immigrants in southwestern Ontario. C

386 Kovacs, Martin L. *Esterhazy and Early Hungarian Immigration to Canada: A Study Based upon the Esterhazy Immigration Pamphlet.* Regina: University of Regina, Canadian Plains Research Centre, 1974, 170 pp., paper.

"This volume is concerned with the pamphlet (1902) compiled by Esterhazy as a result of his visit to the Esterhaz Colony, the first Hungarian-Canadian settlement in what today is the Province of Saskatchewan." D

HUTTERITES

387 Barass, Georgeen. "Hutterites–the Peaceful People." *Canadian Collector*, January/February 1976, pp. 77-79.

The history and contemporary life of Hutterites. C

388 Barnett, Don C., and Knight, Lowry P. *The Hutterite People: A Religious Community.* Saskatoon: Western Extension College, 1977, 71 pp., paper.

Designed for use in elementary classrooms. A

389 Flint, David. *The Hutterites: A Study in Prejudice.* Toronto: Oxford University Press, 1975, 193 pp., paper.

A text designed for high school use. Flint discusses the European and North American history of the Hutterites, their relationships with the larger society, and the contemporary life of a colony in Pincher Creek, Alberta. C

390 Gross, Paul S. *The Hutterite Way: The Inside Story of the Life, Customs, Religion, and Traditions of the Hutterites.* Saskatoon: Freeman Publishing, 1965, 219 pp., cloth.

The author, a Hutterite, writes of the group's culture from the perspective of the group. D

391 Homewood, E. L. "The Hutterites: How Not to Win Friends." *Observer* (United Church), January 1973, pp. 30-33.

The way of life of the Hutterites. C

392 *The Hutterites* (motion picture). Directed by Colin Low. Montreal: National Film Board, 1964. (16mm, 27 min., black and white)

An introduction to Hutterite culture and history.

393 Knill, William D. "Hutterites: Cultural Transmission in a Closed Society." *Alberta Historical Review*, vol. 16, no. 3, 1968, pp. 1-10.

Knill discusses Hutterite training of their young and in so doing reveals important aspects of their culture and social patterns. D

394 MacDonald, Robert J. "Hutterite Education in Alberta: A Test Case in Assimilation, 1920-70." *Canadian Ethnic Studies*, vol. 8, no. 1, 1976, pp. 9-22. D

395 Palmer, Howard. "The Hutterite Land Expansion Controversy in Alberta." *Western Canadian Journal of Anthropology*, vol. 2, no. 2, 1971, pp. 18-46. D

396 Peters, Victor. "The Hutterians: History and Communal Organization of a Rural Group." In *Historical Essays on the Prairie Provinces*, pp. 131-41. Edited by Donald Swainson. Toronto: McClelland and Stewart, 1970, paper.

The history and contemporary life of Hutterites. D

397 Russell, George. "Bound Together in the Fear of a Harsh God." *Weekend Magazine*, 6 April 1974, pp. 2-4.

Discusses the Hutterite way of life and their ability to prevent social and cultural change. C

398 Sawka, Patricia. "The Hutterian Way of Life." *Canadian Geographical Journal*, October 1968, pp. 126-31. C

399 Schmidt, John. "Hutterites Have a Commune That Works." *Canada and the World*, November 1971, pp. 6-7. B

ICELANDERS (See also Scandinavians)

400 "Canadian Scene: Celebrating the Icelandic Fact." *Time*, 11 August 1975, pp. 8-9.

A description of the celebrations commemorating 100 Years of Icelandic settlement in Canada. C

401 Elford, Jean. "The Icelanders—Their Ontario Year." *Beaver*, Spring 1974, pp. 53-58.

The Icelanders who settled in Gimli, Manitoba, spent their first year in Canada in Ontario before moving westward. C

402 *Icelandic Canadian.* Quarterly.

Each issue contains a variety of articles relating to Icelandic Canadian history and culture.

403 Matthiasson, John S. "Icelandic Canadians in Central Canada; One Experiment in Multiculturalism." *Western Canadian Journal of Anthropology*, vol. 4, no. 2, 1974, pp. 49-61.

The author explores three themes: Icelandic history, Icelandic-Canadian history, and cultural activities among Icelandic Canadians. D

INDIANS (See also Native Peoples)

404 *Age of the Buffalo* (motion picture). Directed by Austin Campbell. Montreal: National Film Board, 1964. (16mm and 35 mm, 14 min., color)

The role of the buffalo in the Indian way of life.

405 Ahenakew, Edward. *Voices of the Plains Cree.* Edited and with an introduction by Ruth M. Buck. Toronto: McClelland and Stewart, 1973, 200 pp., paper.

The history, traditional culture, and changing way of life of the Plains Cree. The time period is the mid-1800s to the 1920s. C

406 Badcock, William T. *Who Owns Canada?: Aboriginal Title and Canadian Courts.* Ottawa: Canadian Association in Support of the Native Peoples, 1976, 42 pp., paper. D

407 *The Ballad of Crowfoot* (motion picture). Directed by Willie Dunn. Montreal: National Film Board, 1968. (16mm and 35mm, 10 min., black and white)

An Indian perspective on the opening of the Canadian West.

408 Bauer, George W. "Aboriginal Rights in Canada." *Canadian Forum*, May 1973, pp. 15-20.

An examination of the Indian land claims question. C

409 ——. "Cree Way." *North*, September/October 1977, pp. 6-11.

The author blends three topics: a case study of the concerns of one man, Indian history, and the education program being developed by the Cree of Rupert House, Quebec. C

410 ——. "A Dance to Honour the Sun." *Saturday Night*, September 1972, pp. 19-21.

The annual Sun Dance on the Poorman's Reserve in Saskatchewan. C

411 ——. "James Bay: The Last Massacre of Indian Rights." *Saturday Night*, January 1973, pp. 15-19. C

412 Bowles, Richard P.; Hanley, J. L.; Hodgins, B. W.; and Rawlyk, G. A., eds. *The Indian: Assimilation, Integration or Separation?* Scarborough: Prentice-Hall, 1972, 248 pp., paper.

An edited book designed for classroom use. It includes sections on contemporary Indians, their history, Indian-white relations, and what the future could and/or will bring. C

413 *By Instinct a Painter* (motion picture). Directed by William Zborowsky. Toronto: Canadian Broadcasting Corporation, 1976. (16mm, 23 min., color) Distributor: National Film Board.

Cree artist Allan Sapp.

414 Campbell, Maria. *People of the Buffalo: How the Plains Indians Lived.* Vancouver: J. J. Douglas, 1976, 32 pp., cloth.

Well illustrated. A

415 Canada. Department of Indian and Northern Affairs. Indian and Eskimo Affairs Program. *About Indians: A Listing of Books.* 3d ed. Ottawa: Information Canada, 1975, 321 pp., free. Distributor: Department of Indian and Northern Affairs.

416 *Canada and the World.* September 1975, Special Issue: Native Peoples.

A feature issue with articles on Indian origins, the Beothucks, the Indian Act, aboriginal rights, education, and reserves. B

417 *The Canadian Indian Nations* (audiotape). Toronto: Canadian Broadcasting Corporation, 1971. (30 min.)

Indians before the arrival of the white man, and the cultural future of Canada's Indians.

418 Cardinal, Harold. *The Rebirth of Canada's Indians.* Edmonton: Hurtig, 1977, 222 pp., paper and cloth.

Cardinal sees new hope for Indian people as they progressively take greater control of their own destiny. D

419 ——. *The Unjust Society: The Tragedy of Canada's Indians.* Edmonton: Hurtig, 1969, 171 pp., paper.

An analysis of the problems facing Canada's Indians from both a contemporary and a historical perspective. D

420 *César's Bark Canoe* (motion picture). Directed by Bernard Gosselin. Montreal: National Film Board, 1971. (16mm, 57 min., color)

César Newashish, a Cree, produces a birchbark canoe in the traditional way.

421 Chalmers, John W. "Treaty No. Six." *Alberta History*, vol. 25, no. 2, Spring 1977, pp. 23-27. D

422 *Charley Squash Goes to Town* (motion picture). Directed by Duke Redbird. Montreal: National Film Board, 1969. (16mm, 4 min., color)

An animated film about an Indian leaving his reserve for the city.

423 Cheda, Sherrill. "Indian Women: An Historical Example and a Contemporary View." In *Women in Canada*, pp. 195-208. Edited by Marylee Stephenson. Don Mills: General Publishing, 1977, paper. D

424 *Childhood on an Indian Reservation* (audiotape). Toronto: Canadian Broadcasting Corporation, 1972. (30 min.)

Interviews with Indians who grew up on reserves.

425 *The Colors of Pride* (motion picture). Montreal: National Film Board, 1973. (16mm, 27 min., color)

Four Indian painters.

426 *A Conversation with Duke Redbird* (audiotape). Toronto: Canadian Broadcasting Corporation, 1968. (60 min.)

A discussion with Redbird about the communication problems between whites and Indians.

427 *A Corn Husk Doll, by Deanna Skye* (motion picture). Directed by Geoff Voyce. Ottawa: B. T. Film-Sound, n.d. (16mm, 11 min., color) Distributor: North American Indian Films.

Ms. Skye produces a corn husk doll, a common toy in Indian cultures.

428 *Cree Hunters of Mistassini* (motion picture). Directed by Tony Ianuzielo and Boyce Richardson. Montreal: National Film Board, 1974. (16mm, 57 min., color)

The life of the Cree hunters of northern Quebec during the winter months.

429 *The Cree of Paint Hills* (motion picture). Directed by Diederick d'Ailly. Toronto: Canadian Broadcasting Corporation, 1976. (56 min., color) Distributor: National Film Board.

Cultural preservation among the Cree of James Bay.

430 Dempsey, Hugh A. "The Centennial of Treaty Seven and Why Indians Think Whites Are Knaves." *Canadian Geographical Journal*, October/November 1977, pp. 10-19. C

431 Dingman, Elizabeth. "Indian Women—Most Unequal in Canada." *Chatelaine*, February 1973, pp. 38-39. C

432 Doerr, Audrey D. "The Dilemma of Indian Policy in Canada." *Quarterly of Canadian Studies for the Secondary School*, vol. 3, no. 4, 1975, pp. 198-207. D

433 Dosman, Edgar J. *Indians: The Urban Dilemma*. Toronto: McClelland and Stewart, 1972, 192 pp., paper.

"The purpose of the book is to study the apparent failure, so far, of attempts to arrest the growth of Indian poverty in Canadian cities." D

434 Dunn, Marty. *Red on White: The Biography of Duke Redbird*. Toronto: New Press, 1970, 121 pp., cloth.

435 Eisenberg, John, and Troper, Harold. *Native Survival.* Toronto: Ontario Institute for Studies in Education, 1973, 99 pp., paper.

This book, designed for high school use, is an excellent series of case studies with issues, questions, and analogies. C

436 Escott, Manny. "Playing the White Man's Game—and Winning." *Maclean's*, 12 January 1976, p. 49.

A cross-Canada survey of Indian business ventures. C

437 Ferrante, Angela. "Condemned of Kaboni." *Maclean's*, January 1976, p. 17.

An examination of the high suicide rate among young Ojibway on a Manitoulin Island reserve. C

438 Frideres, James S. *Canada's Indians: Contemporary Conflicts.* Scarborough, Ont.: Prentice-Hall, 1974, 209 pp., paper and cloth. D

439 Fumoleau, Rene OMI. *As Long as This Land Shall Last: A History of Treaty 8 and Treaty 11. 1870-1939.* Toronto: McClelland and Stewart, 1975, 415 pp., paper. C

440 ——. "Treaties: A History of Exploitation." *Canadian Forum*, November 1976, pp. 17-20.

Extracts from Father Fumoleau's testimony to the Berger Commission. C

441 George, Chief Dan, and Hirnschall, Helmut. *My Heart Soars.* Saanichton, B.C.: Hancock House, 1974, 95 pp., cloth.

The writings of Chief Dan George, mostly poetry, are accompanied by illustrations by Hirnschall. A

442 *God Help the Man Who Would Part with His Land* (motion picture). Directed by George C. Stoney. Montreal: National Film Board, 1971. (16mm, 46 min., black and white)

Mohawk Indians contest white people's claim to two islands in the St. Lawrence.

443 Gooderham, Kent, ed. *I Am an Indian.* Toronto: Dent, 1969, 196 pp., cloth.

An anthology of works by Indian authors. Prepared for school use. B

444 Graham, Elizabeth. *Medicine Man to Missionary: Missionaries as Agents of Change among the Indians of Southern Ontario, 1784-1867.* Toronto: Peter Martin Associates, 1975, 110 pp., paper and cloth. D

445 Hagan, John. "Locking up the Indians: A Case for Law Reform." *Canadian Forum*, February 1976, pp. 16-18.

Recommendations for reforming the judicial system so that Canadian prisons will no longer be "filled in large numbers with Native persons convicted of minor charges." D

446 *Haida Carver* (motion picture). Directed by Richard Gilbert. Montreal: National Film Board, 1974. (16mm, 12 min., color)

A young Haida carver produces miniature totems from argillite.

447 Hardwick, Francis C., ed. *When Strangers Meet: A Sourcebook for the Study of a Meeting between Two Cultures.* 2d ed. Vancouver: Tantalus Research, 1974, 82 pp., paper.

The meeting of Europeans and Indians. Extensive use of primary source material. B

448 Hoople, Joanne, and Newberry, J. W. E. *And What about Canada's Native Peoples?* 2d ed. Ottawa: Canadian Council for International Cooperation, 1976, 48 pp., paper.

A brief survey of contemporary Indian problems and concerns. An examination of the parallels between Canada's Native Peoples and the peoples of the Third World is presented. C

449 Howley, James P. *The Beothucks or Red Indians.* 1915. Reprint ed. Rexdale, Ont.: Coles, 1974, 448 pp., paper and cloth. D

450 *Indian Control of Indian Education.* Ottawa: National Indian Brotherhood, 1972, 38 pp., paper. D

451 *Indian News.* English and French, monthly, free.

Published by the Department of Indian and Northern Affairs.

452 *The Indian Speaks* (motion picture). Directed by Marcel Carrière. Montreal: National Film Board, 1967. (16mm and 35mm, 40 min., color)

Indians' concern for the preservation of their culture is examined.

453 *It's Our Move* (motion picture). Montreal: National Film Board, 1973. (16mm, 24 min., color)

A survey of developments taking place on Indian reserves in Ontario.

454 *James Bay* (motion picture). Directed by Diederick d'Ailly. Toronto: Canadian Broadcasting Corporation, 1976. (16mm, 27 min., color) Distributor: National Film Board.

An examination of the environmental and cultural impact of the James Bay power development.

455 Jenness, Diamond. *The Indians of Canada.* 7th ed. Toronto: University of Toronto Press, 1977, 432 pp., paper and cloth.

Perhaps the best scholarly study of pre-contact Indian cultures. D

456 *Joe Jacobs, Stone Carver* (motion picture). Directed by Geoff Voyce. Ottawa: B. T. Film-Sound, n.d. (16mm, 10 min., color) Distributor: North American Indian Films.

457 *Kainai* (motion picture). Directed by Raoul Fox. Montreal: National Film Board, 1973. (16mm, 26 min., color)

Industrial development on the Blood Reserve in Alberta.

458 Kew, Della, and Goddard, P. E. *Indian Art and Culture of the Northwest Coast.* Saanichton, B.C.: Hancock House, 1974, 76 pp., paper.

Pre-contact cultures. Well illustrated. D

459 Kirkness, Verna J. "Programs for Native People by Native People: A Native Perspective." *Education Canada*, vol. 16, no. 4, 1976, pp. 32-35.

An overview of the Indian perspective on education by the Education Director of the National Indian Brotherhood. C

460 Larner, John W.; O'Reilly, James A.; and Brant, Valerie C. *Aboriginal People of Canada and Their Environment.* Ottawa: National Indian Brotherhood, 1973, 22 pp., paper. D

461 Lilley, Wayne. "Canada's Indians: Life Yesterday." *Canada and the World*, February 1974, pp. 20-21. B

462 *The Longhouse People* (motion picture). Montreal: National Film Board, 1951. (16mm, 23 min., color)

This film, originally produced to portray the contemporary culture of the Iroquois, is now of historical significance.

463 Loon, Ken. "Land Lasts Longer Than Money." *Canada and the World*, October 1977, pp. 18-19.

Indian land claims. B

464 McConkey, Lois. *Sea and Cedar: How the Northwest Coast Indians Lived.* Vancouver: J. J. Douglas, 1973, 32 pp., cloth.

Well illustrated. A

465 McFeat, Tom, ed. *Indians of the North Pacific Coast: Studies in Selected Topics.* Toronto: McClelland and Stewart, 1966, 268 pp., paper.

A collection of scholarly papers. E

466 McGee, H. J., ed. *The Native People of Atlantic Canada: A History of Ethnic Interaction.* Toronto: McClelland and Stewart, 1974, 211 pp., paper.

This is a book of readings focussing on the history of Indian-white interaction since the time of the Norsemen. One particularly valuable article examines culture change among the Micmac, based on a comparison of field work done in 1911/12 and 1950. D

467 *A Malecite Fancy Basket* (motion picture). Directed by Geoff Voyce. Ottawa: B. T. Film-Sound, n.d. (16mm, 12 min., color) Distributor: North American Indian Films.

Two Malecite Indians demonstrate basket making.

468 Manuel, George. "Appeal from the Fourth World: The Dene Nation and Aboriginal Rights." *Canadian Forum*, November 1976, pp. 8-12.

Manuel's presentation to the Berger Commission. C

469 Manuel, George, and Posluns, Michael. *The Fourth World: An Indian Reality.* Don Mills: Collier-Macmillan, 1974, 278 pp., paper and cloth. C

470 Marshall, Ingeborg. *The Red Ochre People: How Newfoundland's Beothuck Indians Lived.* Vancouver: J. J. Douglas, 1977, 48 pp., cloth.

Well illustrated. A

471 Mason, Patricia. F. *Indian Tales of the Northwest.* Vancouver: Commcept, 1976, 102 pp., paper.

There is an accompanying teacher's guide. B

472 *A Micmac Scale Basket* (motion picture). Directed by Geoff Voyce. Ottawa: B. T. Film-Sound, n.d. (16mm, 12 min., color) Distributor: North American Indian Films.

Two Micmac Indians demonstrate the production of a basket from raw materials to finished product.

473 *A Moon Mask, by Freda Diesing* (motion picture). Directed by Geoff Voyce. Ottawa: B. T. Film-Sound, n.d. (16mm, 10 min., color) Distributor: North American Indian Films.

Ms. Diesing produces a mask representing the designs and skills of Northwest Coast Indians.

474 Morton, W. L. "Canada and the Canadian Indians: What Went Wrong." *Quarterly of Canadian Studies for the Secondary School,* vol. 2, no. 1, Spring 1972, pp. 3-12. D

475 Nagler, Mark. *Natives without a Home.* Don Mills: Longman, 1975, 83 pp., paper.

A study of Indians today. D

476 *The Native Peoples of North America* (filmstrip). Toronto: Moreland-Latchford, n.d. 6 filmstrips (color), 6 cassettes, and 1 guide.

A historical series which explores pre-contact and post-contact Indian life. There are two filmstrips on each of the following culture areas: Pacific Northwest, Northeastern Woodlands, and Great Plains.

477 *The Other Side of the Ledger: An Indian View of the Hudson's Bay Company* (motion picture). Directed by Martin Defalco and Willie Dunn. Montreal: National Film Board, 1972. (16mm, 42 min., color)

478 *Our Land Is Our Life* (motion picture). Directed by Tony Ianuzielo and Boyce Richardson. Montreal: National Film Board, 1974. (16mm, 57 min., color)

The Cree of northern Quebec react to the offer of compensation for the destructive effects of the James Bay power development.

479 *A Pair of Moccasins, by Mary Thomas* (motion picture). Directed by Geoff Voyce. Ottawa: B. T. Film-Sound, n.d. (16mm, 15 min., color) Distributor: North American Indian Films.

Ms. Thomas, a Shuswap Indian, demonstrates the production of moccasins from the tanning of the hide to the finished product.

480 Patterson, E. Palmer. *The Canadian Indian: A History since 1500.* Toronto: Collier-Macmillan, 1972, 210 pp., paper and cloth. D

481 Patterson, Palmer, and Patterson, Nancy-Lou. *The Changing People: A History of the Canadian Indians.* Toronto: Collier-Macmillan, 1971, 58 pp., paper. B

482 Pelletier, Wilfred, "Childhood in an Indian Village." *This Magazine Is about Schools*, Spring 1969, pp. 6-22.

An excellent case study of Indian culture. C

483 Pelletier, Wilfred, and Poole, Ted. *No Foreign Land: A Biography of a North American Indian.* Toronto: McClelland and Stewart, 1976, 211 pp., paper.

In addition to being a biography of Pelletier, this book is a moving portrayal of the Indian way of life. B

484 *The People at Dipper* (motion picture). Directed by Richard Gilbert and Jack Ofield. Montreal: National Film Board, 1966. (16mm, 18 min., color)

Life on a Chippewa reserve in northern Saskatchewan.

485 *People of the Sacred Circle* (motion picture). Directed by Sig Gerber. Toronto: Canadian Broadcasting Corporation, 1976. (16mm, 27 min., color) Distributor: National Film Board.

Cultural, especially spiritual, revitalization among Indians of various nations gathered at the Morley Indian Reserve in Alberta for the annual Indian Ecumenical Conference.

486 Persky, Stan. "To Build a Nation Once More: The Rise of Native Militancy in B.C." *This Magazine*, November/December 1974, pp. 3-9. D

487 *Porcupine Quill Work, by Bernadette Pangawish* (motion picture). Directed by Geoff Voyce. Ottawa: B. T. Film-Sound, n.d. (16mm, 10 min., color) Distributor: North American Indian Films.

Ms. Pangawish, an Odawa Indian, is shown decorating a box in a traditional design.

488 Richardson, Boyce. *Strangers Devour the Land: The Cree Hunters of the James Bay Area versus Premier Bourassa and the James Bay Development Corporation.* Toronto: Macmillan, 1976, 330 pp., paper and cloth.

The central focus of the book is the James Bay hydroelectric project. In addition, it provides an excellent portrayal of the culture of the James Bay Cree. D

489 Robertson, Heather. *Reservations Are for Indians.* Toronto: James Lorimer, 1970, 303 pp., paper and cloth. D

490 Rowe, Frederick W. *Extinction: The Beothucks of Newfoundland.* Toronto: McGraw-Hill Ryerson, 1977, 176 pp., cloth.

Rowe sets the study of the Beothucks in clearer focus by dispelling many myths and distortions. D

491 Shumiatcher, Morris C. *Welfare: Hidden Backlash.* Toronto: McClelland and Stewart, 1971, 215 pp., cloth.

Shumiatcher suggests that the obstacles preventing Indian progress and development are the paternalism of government in the past and welfare statism today. D

492 Snow, Chief John. *These Mountains Are Our Sacred Places: The Story of the Stoney Indians.* Toronto: Samuel Stevens, 1977, 186 pp., cloth.

A historical and cultural study of the Stoney people. Chief Snow also discusses the future of his people. C

493 *Standing Buffalo* (motion picture). Directed by Joan Henson. Montreal: National Film Board, 1968. (16mm, 23 min., color)

A rug-making cooperative among the Sioux Indian women on a reserve in southern Saskatchewan.

494 *Starblanket* (motion picture). Directed by Donald Brittain. Montreal: National Film Board, 1973. (16mm, 27 min., color)

Noel Starblanket, a young Indian chief, is featured at work.

495 Surtees, Robert J. *The Original People.* Toronto: Holt, Rinehart and Winston, 1971, 101 pp., paper.

A historical study with extracts from primary sources. C

496 *These Are My People* (motion picture). Directed by Michael Mitchell. Montreal: National Film Board, 1969. (16mm, 13 min., black and white)

Two members of the St. Regis Reserve speak of their culture, history, future, and the impact of the white man.

497 *This Was the Time* (motion picture). Directed by Eugene Boyko. Montreal: National Film Board, 1970. (16mm and 35mm, 15 min., color)

A potlatch among the Haida Indians, the first held in over two generations.

498 *Tony Hunt, Kwakiutl Artist* (motion picture). Directed by Geoff Voyce. Ottawa: B. T. Film-Sound, n.d. (16mm, 10 min., color) Distributor: North American Indian Films.

499 Troyer, Warner. *No Safe Place.* Toronto: Clarke Irwin, 1977, 267 pp., cloth.

A study of mercury pollution in Northwest Ontario and its impact on the Ojibway Indians. D

500 Upton, L. F. S. "Colonists and Micmacs." *Journal of Canadian Studies*, vol. 10, no. 3, 1975, pp. 44-56. D

501 ———. "The Extermination of the Beothucks of Newfoundland." *Canadian Historical Review*, vol. 58, no. 2, 1977, pp. 133-53. D

502 Walsh, Gerald. *Indians in Transition: An Inquiry Approach.* Toronto: McClelland and Stewart, 1971, 200 pp., paper.

A resource book for high school courses. C

503 Ward, Fred. "The Changing World of Canada's Cree." *National Geographic*, April 1975, pp. 541-69.

The contemporary culture of the James Bay Cree. B

504 Watkins, Mel. *Dene Nation: The Colony Within.* Toronto: University of Toronto Press, 1977, 200 pp., paper and cloth.

"This collection of papers . . . has been selected in the main from presentations made to the Berger Inquiry, and reflects the efforts of the Dene people to block the construction of a pipeline through the Mackenzie Valley lands they claim as their own." D

505 Waubageshig, ed. *The Only Good Indian: Essays by Canadian Indians.* Toronto: New Press, 1970, 188 pp., paper and cloth. D

506 White, Charles A. "Canada's Indians: Problems Today." *Canada and the World*, February 1974, pp. 24-25. B

507 Whiteside, Don (sin a paw). *Aboriginal People: A Selected Bibliography Concerning Canada's First People.* Ottawa: National Indian Brotherhood, 1973, 345 pp., paper.

508 *Who Were the Ones?* (motion picture). Directed by Michael Mitchell. Montreal: National Film Board, 1972. (16mm and 35mm, 7 min., color)

This song film presents the Indian view of North American history after the arrival of the white man.

509 Woodcock, George. *Peoples of the Coast: The Indians of the Pacific Northwest.* Edmonton: Hurtig, 1977, 223 pp., cloth.

An authoritative study of the culture of the Northwest Coast Indians before large-scale culture change occurred. D

510 Wuttunee, William I. C. *Ruffled Feathers: Indians in Canadian Society.* 2d ed. Calgary: Bell Books, 1971, paper.

Wuttunee, a Cree Indian and lawyer, disagrees with accepted "truths" about Indians. For example, he is opposed to reserves and Red Power movements and argues for integration of Indians. C

511 *You Are on Indian Land* (motion picture). Directed by Mort Ransen. Montreal: National Film Board, 1969. (16mm, 36 min., black and white)

A demonstration held by the Mohawk Indians of Cornwall, Ontario, protesting customs regulations being applied to them.

INUIT (See also Native Peoples)

512 *Angotee: Story of an Eskimo Boy* (motion picture). Directed by Douglas Wilkinson. Montreal: National Film Board, 1953. (16mm, 31 min., color)

The development of an Inuit male from birth to maturity.

513   Balikci, Asen. *The Netsilik Eskimo.* Toronto: Doubleday, 1972, paper and cloth.

An excellent description of the pre-contact culture of the Netsilik Inuit. C

514   Breummer, Fred. "Forerunners of Summerhill." *North*, September/October 1971, pp. 10-19.

Inuit child-rearing practices. C

515   Brody, Hugh. *The People's Land: Eskimos and Whites in the Eastern Arctic.* Don Mills: Penguin, 1975, 240 pp., paper.

"The nature and consequences of white-Eskimo interaction are at the heart of this book." C

516   Burnford, Sheila. "Pond Inlet." *Maclean's*, February 1973, pp. 30-33.

An Inuit community. C

517   Canada. Department of Indian and Northern Affairs. *Innunnit: The Art of the Canadian Eskimo.* By W. T. Larmour. Ottawa, 1974, 106 pp., paper.

Photographs of sculpture and reproductions of prints with an introductory essay. B

518   Canada. Department of Northern Affairs and Natural Resources. *Canadian Eskimo Art.* Ottawa, 1965, 40 pp., paper.

Well illustrated.

519   Crowe, Keith. "Music of the Canadian Inuit." *North*, November/December 1976, pp. 52-56. C

520   Cutler, Maurice. "New Militance . . . Eskimo Power!" *Business Quarterly*, Autumn 1972, pp. 84-87.

The Inuit Tapirisat of Canada, its organization, leadership, and concerns. C

521   ——. "'Perhaps We Could Have Done Better' Alma Houston." *Business Quarterly*, Autumn 1972, pp. 88-95.

Mrs. Houston, long involved with the production and distribution of Inuit art, comments on the impact of the white man on Inuit culture. C

522   "End of Inuit Camp Life 1950-1976." *North*, July/August 1976, pp. 36-49.

This article presents four views—two white and two Inuit—on the passing of the traditional Inuit culture. C

523   *The Eskimo: Fight for Life* (motion picture). Montreal: National Film Board, 1970. (16mm, 51 min., color)

The traditional way of life of the Netsilik Inuit.

524   *Eskimos Myth and Legends* (kit). Scarborough: ETHOS, 1974. 4 filmstrips, 2 cassettes, 2 teacher's manuals, and reading scripts.

Designed for elementary school use.

525 *Eskimos Stories* (kit). Scarborough: ETHOS, 1974. 4 filmstrips, 2 cassettes, 2 teacher's manuals, and reading scripts.

Designed for elementary school use.

526 French, Alice. *My Name is Lasak.* Winnipeg: Peguis Publishers, 1977, 110 pp., paper and cloth.

The author tells the story of her childhood. B

527 Frere, R. *Eskimo Life of Yesterday.* Saanichton, B.C.: Hancock House, 1977, 48 pp., paper.

Photographs taken in the early 1900s.

528 Hale, Barrie. "The Snow Prints: Inuit Visions in an Adopted Art Form." *Canadian*, 5 June 1976, pp. 8-11.

Inuit printmaking. B

529 Hofmann, Charles. *Drum Dance: Legends, Ceremonies, Dances and Songs of the Eskimos.* Toronto: Gage, 1974, 95 pp., paper and cloth. B

530 *How to Build an Igloo* (motion picture). Directed by Douglas Wilkinson. Montreal: National Film Board, 1950. (16mm, 10 min., color)

531 Hughes, Barry Conn. "The White Man Who Wouldn't Use the Honey Bucket." *Canadian Magazine*, 8 February 1975.

Ten Inuit speak of themselves, their concerns, and their perceptions of white men. B

532 *An Introduction to the Eskimo People of Canada and Their National Organization.* Ottawa: Inuit Tapirisat of Canada, n.d., 33 pp., paper, free.

533 *Inuit Legends* (audiotape). Toronto: Canadian Broadcasting Corporation, 1974/75. (60 min., reel and cassette)

534 *Inuit Today.* English and Inuktitut, monthly.

Published by the Inuit Tapirisat of Canada. Contains news articles about the Inuit and the North as well as an Inuit literary section.

535 Kurelek, William. *The Last of the Arctic.* Toronto: McGraw-Hill Ryerson, 1976, 94 pp., cloth.

Paintings and drawings accompanied by commentaries on the pre-contact Inuit life style. B

536 ———. "The Last of the Arctic: Inuit Life before the Snowmobiles." *Canadian*, 23 October 1976, pp. 8-11.

An extract from Kurelek's book *The Last of the Arctic.* B

537 Moss-Davies, Anthony. "A Hard Winter for the Eskimo Hunter." *Saturday Night*, March 1973, p. 43.

The extreme economic difficulties faced by Inuit who continue to live off the land. C

538 ——. "I Married a Stone Age Woman." *Chatelaine*, January 1976, p. 32.

A humorous article based on the author's experiences, which shattered his myths about a native's—his wife's—"inability" to be successful in white society and the white man's, particularly the author's, supposed superiority. B

539 Netsilik Eskimos Series (motion picture). Montreal: National Film Board, 1967. (16mm, color) 9 films in 21 half-hour parts.

A major study of Inuit culture before significant cultural change occurred.

540 *The Netsilik Eskimo Today* (motion picture). Montreal: National Film Board, 1972. (16mm, 17 min., color)

A case study of a Netsilik Inuit family in a modern settlement.

541 "The North: Goodbye, Dick and Jane." *Time*, 4 February 1974, p. 10.

Changes are taking place in the northern education system to make it more relevant to the Inuit. B

542 "The North: Return to the Land." *Time*, 11 March 1974, p. 10.

Some Inuit have left northern settlements and returned to live off the land. B

543 Nuligak and Metager, Maurice, trans. and ed. *I, Nuligak*. Markham, Ont.: Simon and Schuster, 1971, paper.

The autobiography of Nuligak, who was born in 1895 in the Mackenzie Delta. B

544 O'Connell, Sheldon. "Television's Impact on the Eskimo." *North*, November/December 1975, pp. 34-37. C

545 *People of the Seal: Part 1–Eskimo Summer and Part 2–Eskimo Winter* (motion picture). Montreal: National Film Board, 1971. (16 mm, 51 min. each, color)

A two-part series based on the longer Netsilik Eskimo Series.

546 *Pictures out of My Life* (motion picture). Directed by Zina Heczko. Montreal: National Film Board, 1973. (16mm and 35mm, 13 min., color)

The work of Pitseolak, an Inuit artist.

547 Pitseolak, Peter. *People from Our Side: An Inuit Record of Seekooselak–The Land and People of Cape Dorset, Baffin Island*. Translated by Ann Hanson. Edmonton: Hurtig, 1975, 159 pp., paper and cloth.

Based on a manuscript by and interviews with Pitseolak, a Baffin Island Inuit in his 70s. Well illustrated with photographs by Pitseolak. B

548 Power, Ann Hervey. *Eskimos of Canada*. Don Mills, Ont.: Collier-Macmillan Canada, 1971, 44 pp., paper.

This booklet concentrates on pre-contact Inuit culture and the impact of the explorers, whalers, traders, missionaries, and representatives of government. A short section is devoted to the Inuit today. B

549 Pryde, Duncan. *Nunaga: Ten Years of Eskimo Life.* New York: Bantam Books, 1971, 309 pp., paper.

Pryde describes his experiences in the Canadian north as a fur trader. The last chapter, "The Changing Arctic," examines social and cultural change among the Inuit. C

550 Rowley, G. W. "What Are Eskimos?" *Canada and the World*, February 1974, pp. 20-21. B

551 *Sananguagat: Inuit Masterworks* (motion picture). Directed by Derek May. Montreal: National Film Board, 1974. (16mm and 35mm, 24 min., color)

Inuit carvings.

552 Smith, E. J., and Handley, J. L. *The Inuit: A Model for Survival.* Eskimo Point, N.W.T.: Inuit Cultural Institute, 1975, 23 pp., free.

A resource book for teachers preparing curricula on the Inuit.

553 *Spirit in a Landscape: The People Beyond* (motion picture). Directed by Carol Myers. Toronto: Canadian Broadcasting Corporation, 1976. (16mm, 56 min., color) Distributor: National Film Board.

A portrayal of the Inuit with three themes: the physical environment in which they live, their spiritual world, and the impact of change on the Inuit culture.

554 *Stories from Pangnirtung.* Edmonton: Hurtig, 1976, 100 pp., cloth.

Eleven stories as told by Inuit elders. A

555 Thomas, David. "Meeting on the Tundra." *Maclean's*, 31 October 1977, p. 42b.

Quebec Inuit opposition to Bill 101. C

556 Thrasher, Anthony Apakark; Deagle, Gerard; and Merrick, Alan. *Thrasher . . . Skid Row Eskimo.* Toronto: Griffin House, 1976, 164 pp., cloth.

Through the story of one man, Thrasher, the nature of change and its impact on the Inuit are revealed. C

557 Valentine, Victor F., and Vallee, Frank G., eds. *Eskimo of the Canadian Arctic.* Toronto: McClelland and Stewart, 1968, paper.

A collection of scholarly articles. E

558 *We Don't Live in Snow Houses Now: Reflections of Arctic Bay.* Ottawa: Canadian Arctic Producers, 1976, 196 pp., English and Inuktitut, paper. Distributor: Hurtig.

The Inuit of Arctic Bay tell their own story about the changes they have experienced. Well illustrated with photographs. Excellent for classroom use. B

559 *Yesterday–Today–The Netsilik Eskimo* (motion picture). Directed by Gilles Blais. Montreal: National Film Board, 1971. (16mm, 57 min., color)

A contrast of the traditional Inuit way of life with life in modern settlements.

IRISH (See also British)

560 Duncan, Kenneth. "Irish Famine Immigration and the Social Structure of Canada West." In *Studies in Canadian Social History*, pp. 140-63. Edited by Michael Horn and Ronald Sabourin. Toronto: McClelland and Stewart, 1974, paper. D

561 Harris, R. Cole; Roulston, Pauline; and De Freitas, Chris. "Settlement of Mono Township." *Canadian Geographer*, vol. 19, no. 1, 1975, pp. 1-17.

A study from the perspective of historical geography of Irish settlement of Mono Township, Ontario, in the first half of the 1800s. D

562 *Ireland* (motion picture or videocassette). Toronto: CTV Television, n.d. (16mm, or 3/4" videocassette, 50 min., color)

A study of family life in Ireland in relation to Irish Canadians.

563 LeBlanc, J. Leonard. "Peace and Prosperity." *Canada and the World*, October 1976, pp. 14-15.

A brief history of Ireland and Irish immigrants in Canada. B

564 Mannion, John J. *Irish Settlements in Eastern Canada.* Toronto: University of Toronto Press, 1973, 240 pp., paper. D

565 Nemec, Thomas F. "The Irish Emigration to Newfoundland." *Newfoundland Quarterly (Aspects)*, vol. 69, no. 1, 1972, pp. 15-19, 22-24. D

ITALIANS

566 *Bibliography of Centre Material on the Italian Community.* Toronto: Cross-Cultural Communication Centre, n.d., 5 pp., mimeo, free.

567 Boissevain, Jeremy. *The Italians of Montreal: Social Adjustment in a Plural Society.* Ottawa: Information Canada, 1970, 87 pp., paper.

Report of a research study of the social world of Montreal's Italian community and its relations with the English and French communities. D

568 de Villiers, Marq. "Farewell to Little Italy." *Toronto Life*, July 1977, pp. 43-49.

An excellent article which presents an up-to-date view of the Italian community and shatters many stereotypes. C

569 Guiliano, Bruce B. *Sacro O Profano? A Consideration of Four Italian-Canadian Religious Festivals.* Ottawa: National Museum of Man, Canadian Centre for Folk Culture Studies, 1976, 64 pp., paper. D

570 Hardwick, Francis C., ed. *From an Antique Land: Italians in Canada.* Vancouver: Tantalus Research, 1977, 88 pp., paper.

A history of Italian Canadians, largely based on extracts from primary and secondary sources. Includes questions and activities. B

571 *The Italian in Transition* (motion picture). Toronto: Ontario Institute for Studies in Education, 1973. (16mm, 26 min., color) Distributor: International Tele-Film Enterprises.

The transition an Italian child experiences upon entering the Canadian school system.

572 *Italy* (motion picture or videocassette). Toronto: CTV Television, n.d. (16mm, or 3/4" videocassette, 50 min., color)

A study of family life in Italy in relation to Italian Canadians.

573 Johnson, Valerie. "Our Isolated Immigrants." *Saturday Night*, February 1971, pp. 16-20.

A study of Toronto's Italian community with references to the Communities in Ottawa, Vancouver, and Montreal. C

574 Ontario. Ministry of Culture and Recreation. Multicultural Development Branch. *Papers on the Italian Community.* Toronto: n.d., 7 pp., free.

An outstanding paper on the cultural dislocation experienced by immigrants. D

575 Russell, George. "The Italians in Canada: Builders of a New Life." *Weekend Magazine*, 5 October 1974, pp. 7-16.

A short article on the history of Canada's Italian Community. Well illustrated. C

576 Taylor, Rupert J. "Discoverers and City Dwellers." *Canada and the World*, October 1976, p. 22.

A one-page introduction to the Italian community in Canada. B

577 *The Visit* (motion picture). Directed by Bernard Devlin. Montreal: National Film Board, 1964. (16mm, 27 min., black and white)

An Italian immigrant realizes that Canada is home after a trip to his homeland.

JAPANESE (See also Orientals)

578 Adachi, Ken. *The Enemy That Never Was: A History of the Japanese Canadians.* Toronto: McClelland and Stewart, 1976, 456 pp., cloth.

A very comprehensive study. D

579 *Bird of Passage* (motion picture). Directed by Martin Defalco. Montreal: National Film Board, 1966. (16mm, 10 min., black and white)

The life of a Japanese Canadian today, with flashbacks to the events of World War II.

580 Broadfoot, Barry. *Six War Years 1939-1945: Memories of Canadians at Home and Abroad.* Toronto: Doubleday, 1974, pp. 109-119, cloth.

In a chapter entitled "Out with the Japs," Broadfoot presents stories, as told to him by both Japanese and non-Japanese, of the evacuation and relocation of the Japanese. B

581 ———. *Years of Sorrow, Years of Shame: The Japanese Canadians in World War II.* Toronto: Doubleday, 1977, cloth.

Broadfoot uses the techniques of the oral historian to portray the relocation of the Japanese during World War II. B

582 ———. "Years of Sorrow, Years of Shame: 'Remember, We Were Canadian Citizens.'" *Canadian,* 1 October 1977, pp. 2-7.

Excerpts from *Years of Sorrow, Years of Shame.* B

583 Cushing, Bruce. "Japanese-Canadians: Did Canada Treat Them Fairly during World War II?" *Canada and the World,* February 1974, pp. 26-27. B

584 Dahlie, Jorgen. "The Japanese in B.C.: Lost Opportunity: Some Aspects of the Education of Minorities." *BC Studies,* no. 8, Winter 1970/71, pp. 3-16.

The history of education of the Japanese, 1920s-1940s. D

585 *Enemy Alien* (motion picture). Directed by Jeanette Lerman. Montreal: National Film Board, 1975. (16mm and 35mm, 26 min., color)

The relocation of Japanese Canadians during World War II.

586 Henry, Franklin J. *The Experience of Discrimination: A Case Study Approach.* San Francisco: R and E Research Associates, 1974, 104 pp., paper.

A study, conducted in 1964, of discrimination as experienced by the Blacks and Japanese of Hamilton, Ontario. D

587 Iwaasa, David B. "The Japanese in Southern Alberta, 1941-45." *Alberta History,* vol. 24, no. 3, 1976, pp. 5-19. D

588 *Japan* (motion picture or videocassette). Toronto: CTV Television, n.d. (16mm, or 3/4" videocassette, 50 min., color)

A study of family life in Japan in relation to Japanese Canadians.

589 Knight, Rolf, and Koizumi, Maya. *A Man of Our Times: The Life-History of a Japanese-Canadian Fisherman.* Vancouver: New Star Books, 1977, 135 pp., paper and cloth. B

590 La Violette, Forrest E. *The Canadian Japanese and World War II: A Sociological and Psychological Account.* 1948. Reprint ed. Toronto: University of Toronto Press, 1974, 332 pp., cloth. D

591 Marlatt, Daphne, ed. *Steveston Recollected: A Japanese-Canadian History.* Victoria: Provincial Archives of British Columbia, Aural History, 1975, 104 pp., paper.

Oral history. Well illustrated. C

592 Moritsugu, Frank. "The Evacuation." In *Canadians at War: 1939/45*, pp. 151-59. Edited by Douglas How, George Ronald, and Charles Smith. Montreal: Reader's Digest, 1969, cloth. C

593 *The New Canadian.* English and Japanese, semiweekly.

A newspaper carrying both news from Japan and articles about the Japanese-Canadian community.

594 Ontario Human Rights Commission. *A Brief Pictorial Account of Japanese Canadians in Ontario.* Toronto: n.d., n.p., free.

595 Patton, Janice. *The Exodus of the Japanese.* Toronto: McClelland and Stewart, 1973, 47 pp., paper.

An excellent examination of the relocation of the Japanese Canadians. Quotations from Japanese Canadians and period photographs are interspersed throughout the text. C

596 *Rikka.* Quarterly.

Features literary works and articles about the Japanese-Canadian community, other ethnic groups, immigration, and multiculturalism.

597 Roy, Patricia. "The Evacuation of the Japanese, 1942." In *Documentary Problems in Canadian History.* Vol. 2, pp. 215-40. Edited by J. M. Bumstead. Georgetown, Ont.: Irwin-Dorsey, 1969.

A collection of primary sources. C

598 Sagi, Douglas. "No Anger. Not Anymore." *Canadian Magazine*, 27 November 1971, pp. 16-23.

The relocation of Japanese Canadians and their internment in New Denver, B.C. B

599 Takashima, Shizuye. *A Child in Prison Camp.* Montreal: Tundra Books, 1971, n.p., cloth.

With poetry and paintings the author presents, through her own eyes as a child, the evacuation and internment of Japanese Canadians during World War II. B

600 Ward, W. Peter. "British Columbia and the Japanese Evacuation." *Canadian Historical Review*, vol. 57, no. 3, 1976, pp. 290-308. D

JEWS

601 Arnold, A. J. "The Earliest Jews in Winnipeg 1874-1882." *Beaver*, Autumn 1974, pp. 4-11. D

602 ———. "Jewish Pioneer Settlements." *Beaver*, Autumn 1975, pp. 20-26.

Jewish farm settlements in Western Canada. D

603 Chiel, Arthur A. *The Jews in Manitoba.* 1961. Reprint ed. Toronto: University of Toronto Press, 1974, 184 pp., cloth.

604 Hayes, Saul. "Canadian Jewish Culture: Some Observations." *Queen's Quarterly*, vol. 84, no. 1, 1977, pp. 80–88.

An essay on Jewish involvement in the arts. D

605 *Jewish Historical Society of Canada Journal.* Semiannual.

A scholarly journal.

606 "Jews in Canada: Glimpses of Life and Heritage." *Weekend Magazine*, 18 September 1976, pp. 4-6.

Features reproductions, with accompanying short articles, of paintings by Kurelek. D

607 *The Jews of Winnipeg* (motion picture). Directed by Bill Davies. Montreal: National Film Board, 1973. (16mm, 27 min., color)

The history and contemporary life of Winnipeg's Jewish community.

608 Kurelek, William, and Arnold, Abraham. *Jewish Life in Canada.* Edmonton: Hurtig, 1976, 96 pp., cloth.

This book is composed of paintings and commentaries by Kurelek and a historical essay by Arnold. C

609 Levin, Arthur. "A Soviet Jewish Family Comes to Calgary." *Canadian Ethnic Studies*, vol. 6, nos. 1/2, 1974, pp. 53-66.

The family left the USSR in 1972. Interesting presentation of the immigrant experience. E

610 *The People of the Book* (motion picture). Directed by Felix Lazarus. Montreal: National Film Board, 1973. (16mm, 28 min., color)

Religious observance and cultural preservation among Canada's Jews.

611 Plaut, W. Gunther. *Your Neighbor Is a Jew.* Toronto: McClelland and Stewart, 1967, 142 pp., cloth. D

612 Richtik, J., and Hutch, D. "When Jewish Settlers Farmed in Manitoba's Interlake Area." *Canadian Geographical Journal*, August/September 1977, pp. 32-35.

This settlement, Bender Hamlet, was founded in 1902 and prospered for 20 years before it was abandoned. C

613 Rosenberg, Stuart E. *The Jewish Community in Canada.* 2 vols. Toronto: McClelland and Stewart, 1970 and 1971, 240 pp. and 224 pp., cloth.

Vol. I—A history of the Jewish community from its origins in the 1750s to the present. Vol. II—The Jewish community today and Jewish involvement, past and present, in the military, sports, performing arts, writing, and the academic world. D

614 ——. *To Understand Jews: A People, a Culture, a Religion.* Don Mills: Paperjacks, 1972, 159 pp., paper. D

615 Sack, B. G. *History of the Jews in Canada.* Montreal: Harvest House, 1965, 299 pp., cloth. D

616 Sevitt, Carol. "An Ancient Prejudice." *Canada and the World*, December 1977, pp. 18-19.

Anti-Semitism. B

617 Shaffir, William. *Life in a Religious Community: The Lubavitcher Chassidim in Montreal.* Toronto: Holt, Rinehart and Winston, 1974, 244 pp., paper. E

618 *Viewpoints: Canadian Jewish Quarterly.* Vol. 7, nos. 3/4, 1973. Special Issue: The Jews of Canada.

Historical articles on the Jewish community in five regions: Maritimes, Quebec, Ontario, Prairies, and British Columbia. C

619 *Whatever Happened to "Kosher"?* (audiotape). Toronto: Canadian Broadcasting Corporation, n.d. (60 min., reel and cassette)

The kosher custom and its disappearance among Jews.

KOREANS

620 Duncan, Muriel. "The New Ethnic Church." *Observer* (United Church), June 1976, pp. 28-30. B

MACEDONIANS

621 Petroff, L. "Macedonians: From Village to City." *Canadian Ethnic Studies*, vol. 9, no. 1, 1977, pp. 29-41.

"This paper describes the attempt to Canadianize Toronto's Macedonians, and the response of the early Macedonian community to the churches, schools, and health officials who were the agents of that attempt." D

MENNONITES

622 Alderman, Tom. "Yesterday, Today and Tomorrow: For the Old Order Mennonites, They're All the Same." *Canadian Magazine*, 23 August 1975, pp. 8-13. B

623 *And When Their Time Had Come* (motion picture). Waterloo, Ont.: Mennonite Historical Society of Ontario, n.d. (16mm, 45 min., black and white)

This film portrays the history of a Mennonite family, their emigration from Russia, and their settling on a homestead in northern Alberta.

624 Bargen, Peter F. "Mennonite Settlements in Alberta." In *The Pioneer West*, no. 2, pp. 26-31. Calgary: Historical Society of Alberta, 1970, paper. C

625 Davies, Blodwen. *A String of Amber: The Heritage of the Mennonites.* Vancouver: Mitchell Press, 1973, 288 pp., cloth.

A history of the Mennonites in Ontario. Emphasis is placed on Mennonite customs.

Some insights into contemporary Mennonite social patterns and culture are provided. The European history and religious history of the Mennonites are described. C

626 Epp, Frank H. *Mennonites in Canada, 1786-1920: The History of a Separate People.* Toronto: Macmillan, 1974, 480 pp., cloth.

Epp discusses the origin of Mennonites as a part of the Anabaptist movement in Europe; various waves of immigration to Ontario, Manitoba, Alberta, and Saskatchewan; majority-minority relations; and differentiation. D

627 Friesen, William. "A Mennonite Community in the East Reserve: Its Origin and Growth." In *Historical Essays on the Prairie Provinces*, pp. 99-119. Edited by Donald Swainson. Toronto: McClelland and Stewart, 1970.

East Reserve is in Manitoba. C

628 Klippenstein, LaVerna, and Klippenstein, Lawrence. *Rosenort: A Mennonite Community—Book Two: The Growing Years.* Morris, Man.: Morris Macdonald School Division, 1975, 30 pp., paper. Distributor: Conference of Mennonites in Canada.

Prepared for classroom use. A

629 ——. *Rosenort: A Mennonite Community—Book Three: The People Now.* Morris, Man.: Morris Macdonald School Division, 1976, 34 pp., paper. Distributor: Conference of Mennonites in Canada.

Prepared for classroom use. A

630 Klippenstein, Lawrence, ed. "A Visit to Manitoba in 1873: The Russian Mennonite Delegation." *Canada: An Historical Magazine*, September 1975, pp. 48-61. C

631 Klippenstein, Lawrence, and Klippenstein, LaVerna. *Mennonites in Manitoba: Their Background and Early Settlement.* Morris, Man.: Morris Macdonald School Division, 1976, 30 pp., paper. Distributor: Conference of Mennonites in Canada.

Prepared for classroom use. A

632 Klippenstein, Lawrence, and Toews, Julius G., ed. *Mennonite Memories: Settling in Western Canada.* Winnipeg: Centennial Publications, 1977, 340 pp., cloth.

A comprehensive source book. C

633 Mage, Julius, and Murdie, Robert. "The Mennonites of Waterloo County." *Canadian Geographical Journal*, vol. 80, no. 1, 1970, pp. 10-19.

The history and culture of the Old Order Mennonites. D

634 *Mennonite Historian.* Quarterly, free.

A newsletter.

635 *Plain People* (motion picture). Directed by Chip Young. Toronto: Canadian Broadcasting Corporation, 1976. (16mm, 27 min., color) Distributor: National Film Board.

The way of life of the Old Order Mennonites.

636 Redekop, Calvin Wall. *The Old Colony Mennonites: Dilemmas of Ethnic Minority Life.* Baltimore: Johns Hopkins University Press, 1969, 302 pp., cloth.

A study based on participant observation among Old Colony Mennonites in Mexico and Canada. E

637 Staebler, Edna. *Sauerkraut and Enterprise.* Toronto: McClelland and Stewart, 1969, 96 pp., paper.

This fascinating and highly personal little book gives the reader an excellent introduction to Old Order Mennonite and Amish cultures. B

638 Thackeray, Douglas. "The Quiet of the Land." *Harrowsmith*, July/August 1977, pp. 50-61.

The way of life of the Old Order Mennonites. B

METIS (See also Native Peoples)

639 Adams, Howard. "We Must See Our History through Native Eyes." *This Magazine*, June 1974, pp. 19-21.

This article presents an alternative point of view by an outspoken Métis leader. D

640 Bowsfield, Hartwell. *Louis Riel: The Rebel and the Hero.* Toronto: Oxford University Press, 1971, 160 pp., paper. C

641 Brasser, T. J. "Métis Artisans." *Beaver*, Autumn 1975, pp. 52-56. D

642 Campbell, Maria. *Halfbreed.* Toronto: McClelland and Stewart, 1973, 157 pp., paper and cloth.

An autobiography by a noted Métis author. C

643 Carpenter, Jock. *Fifty Dollar Bride: Marie Rose Smith—A Chronicle of Métis Life in the 19th Century.* Sidney, B.C.: Gray's Publishing, 1977, 160 pp., paper.

A biography. B

644 Charlebois, Peter. *The Life of Louis Riel.* Toronto: NC Press, 1975, 256 pp., paper and cloth.

A popular biography. Well illustrated. D

645 Dhand, H.; Hunt, L.; and Goshawk, L. *Louis Riel: An Annotated Bibliography.* Saskatoon: University of Saskatchewan, College of Education, Research Resources Centre, 1972, 41 pp., paper. Distributor: University of Saskatchewan Bookstore.

In addition to suggesting a wide variety of sources on Riel and the Rebellions, this bibliography provides references on the early history of the Métis. Some references are classified according to vocabulary and grade level.

646 Dorge, Lionel. "The Métis and Canadien Councillors of Assiniboia." *Beaver*, Part 1, Summer 1974, pp. 12-19; Part 2, Autumn 1974, pp. 39-45; Part 3, Winter 1974, pp. 51-59.

Examines Métis and Canadien involvement in the Council of Assiniboia, the governing body of the Red River Settlement, 1835-1970. D

647 Flanagan, T. E. "The Religion of Louis Riel." *Quarterly of Canadian Studies for the Secondary School*, vol. 4, no. 1, 1975, pp. 3-14. D

648 Grescoe, Paul. "Back to Batoche: Learning to Be Proud of Mixed Blood." *Canadian Magazine*, 9 March 1974, p. 17.

The annual Back to Batoche celebrations in Batoche, Saskatchewan. B

649 *The Hard Times of Louis Riel* (kit). Scarborough: Prentice-Hall Media, 1977. 2 filmstrips, 2 cassettes, 1 teacher's guide.

650 Howard, Joseph. *Strange Empire: Louis Riel and the Métis People.* Toronto: James Lewis and Samuel, 1974, 601 pp., paper.

A biography of Riel and a history of the Métis people. C

651 Howard, Richard. *Riel.* Toronto: Clarke Irwin, 1967.

One of the Canadian Jackdaws series. B

652 *Like the Trees* (motion picture). Montreal: National Film Board, 1974. (16mm, 14 min., color)

An urban Métis woman discovers her heritage among the Cree of northern Alberta.

653 Neering, Rosemary. *Louis Riel.* Don Mills: Fitzhenry and Whiteside, 1977, 64 pp. B

654 Overvold (Burger), Joanne, ed. *Our Métis Heritage: A Portrayal.* Yellowknife: Métis Association of the Northwest Territories, 1976, 142 pp., cloth.

A pictorial history.

655 Pearl, Stanley. *Louis Riel.* 2d ed. Toronto: Maclean-Hunter Learning Materials, 1972, 64 pp., paper. B

656 Robertson, Heather. "On the Road to Nowhere." *Saturday Night*, August 1970, p. 17.

Ms. Robertson describes "Squatterville," a Métis community in Manitoba, "typical of many Métis communities in the West." C

657 Sealey, D. Bruce. *Cuthbert Grant and the Métis.* Toronto: Book Society of Canada, 1976, 44 pp., paper. A

658 Sealey, Bruce, ed. *Stories of the Métis.* Winnipeg: Manitoba Métis Federation Press, 1973, 148 pp., paper.

Short stories and short non-fiction essays on the history of the Métis in Manitoba and the Manitoba Métis Federation. A

659 Sealey, D. Bruce, and Lussier, Antoine S. *The Métis: Canada's Forgotten People.* Winnipeg: Manitoba Métis Federation Press, 1975, 200 pp., paper.

A history of the Métis in Manitoba. C

660 Sealey, Bruce, and Sealey, Margaret, eds. *Six Métis Communities.* Winnipeg: Manitoba Métis Federation Press, 1974, 91 pp., paper.

Description of six isolated Métis communities in Manitoba. C

661 Stanley, George F. G. *The Birth of Western Canada: A History of the Riel Rebellions.* Toronto: University of Toronto Press, 1960, 457 pp., paper.

The foremost scholarly study of the Riel Rebellions. E

662 ——. *Louis Riel.* Toronto: McGraw-Hill Ryerson, 1972, paper.

The foremost scholarly biography of Riel. E

663 *This Riel Business* (motion picture). Directed by Ian McLaren. Montreal: National Film Board, 1974. (16mm, 27 min., color)

A film of a stage comedy based on the Riel Rebellion.

664 Truss, Jan. *A Very Small Rebellion.* With an essay by Jack Chambers. Edmonton: J. M. Lebel Enterprises, 1977, 95 pp., paper and cloth.

A historical essay on the Riel Rebellions is interspersed with a novelette about "a very small rebellion" executed by several Métis children in the spirit of Riel. B

665 "The West: 'Canada Deserves Us'." *Time*, 21 January 1974, pp. 6-7.

The problems encountered by Métis. C

666 Woodcock, George. "Dumont and Riel: Hero and Martyr." *Canadian Forum*, October 1975, pp. 13-15.

An excerpt from Woodcock's book *Gabriel Dumont.* D

667 ——. *Gabriel Dumont: The Métis Chief and His Lost World.* Edmonton: Hurtig, 1975, 260 pp., paper and cloth. D

NATIVE PEOPLES (See also Indians, Inuit, and Métis)

668 Adams, Howard. *Prison of Grass: Canada from the Native Point of View.* Toronto: New Press, 1975, 238 pp., cloth. D

669 Berger, Mr. Justice Thomas R. *Northern Frontier, Northern Homeland: The Report of the Mackenzie Valley Pipeline.* Vol. 1. Ottawa: Supply and Services Canada, 1977, 213 pp., paper.

The primary purpose of this volume is, of course, to explore the impact of a pipeline in the Mackenzie Valley. In the process of doing this, the report offers many insights into native cultures and the question of native land claims. Well illustrated. D

670 *C.A.S.N.P. Bulletin.* Quarterly.

Published by the Canadian Association in Support of the Native Peoples. Explores issues of contemporary concern to the Native Peoples.

671 Canada. Department of Indian Affairs and Northern Development. *People of Light and Dark.* Ottawa: Information Canada, 1966, 156 pp., paper.

This book contains many valuable readings about Indians and Inuit. Several of these relate to social and cultural change. D

672 *Canada's North* (kit). Scarborough: Prentice-Hall Media, n.d. 2 filmstrips, 2 cassettes, and 1 teacher's guide.

A chronological history of the North. Filmstrip no. 2 discusses the history of the Native Peoples.

673 Cox, Bruce, ed. *Cultural Ecology: Readings on the Canadian Native Peoples.* Toronto: McClelland and Stewart, 1973, 331 pp., paper.

A collection of scholarly papers examining "the relations between cultural and social arrangements and the environmental settings of various Indian and Eskimo groups." E

674 Crowe, Keith J. *A History of the Original Peoples of Northern Canada.* Montreal: Arctic Institute of North America, McGill-Queen's University Press, 1974, 226 pp., paper and cloth.

Designed as a text for northern native students in the early teenage years. The author surveys the history of the Indians and Inuit from the arrival of man in the Americas to the present. Greatest emphasis is placed on culture contact and culture change. C

675 Cumming, Peter A., and Mickenberg, Neil H., eds. *Native Rights in Canada.* 2d ed. Don Mills: General Publishing, 1972, paper and cloth. D

676 Daniels, Christine, and Christiansen, Ron. *The White Man's Laws.* Edmonton: Hurtig, 1970, 136 pp., paper and cloth.

This book "shows clearly the wide gap between traditional Indian laws and the laws of modern society. It exposes the native perception of modern laws. It explains, in native terms, those modern laws most often encountered by native people." Well illustrated. A

677 Dewdney, Selwyn. *They Shared to Survive: The Native Peoples of Canada.* Toronto: Macmillan, 1975, 220 pp., paper and cloth.

A description of Canada's Native Peoples as they lived during the early stages of their contact with Europeans. B

678 Elliott, Jean Leonard, ed. *Minority Canadians 1: Native Peoples.* Scarborough, Ont.: Prentice-Hall, 1971, 169 pp., paper.

Scholarly article about Indians, Inuit, and Métis. D

679 Embree, Jesse. *Let Us Live: The Native Peoples of Canada.* Toronto: Dent, 1977, 64 pp., paper.

Prepared for classroom use. Emphasizes the history and contemporary life of Canada's Native Peoples. C

680 Erasmus, Peter. *Buffalo Days and Nights.* As told to Henry Thompson. Introduction by Irene Spry. Calgary: Glenbow-Alberta Institute, 1976, 343 pp., cloth.

The life story of Erasmus, a Métis guide, interpreter, traveller, trader, teacher, and mission worker. He lived from 1833 to 1931, and his reminiscences focus on the major events in the West during the second half of the 1800s. C

681 Grescoe, Paul. "A Nation's Disgrace" and "Taking Care of Their Own." *Weekend Magazine*, 23 April 1977, p. 4; 30 April 1977, pp. 18-21.

A national report on Native health care. C

682 *Indian-Inuit Authors: An Annotated Bibliography.* Ottawa: National Library of Canada, 1974, 108 pp., paper. Distributor: Supply and Services Canada.

An excellent bilingual bibliography of books, articles, poetry, songs, addresses, and anthologies by Canadian Indian, Métis, and Inuit authors.

683 La Roque, Emma. *Defeathering the Indian: A Handbook on Native Studies.* Agincourt, Ont.: Book Society of Canada, 1975, 82 pp., paper.

La Roque, a Métis, discusses education from the Native perspective and makes recommendations for educators working with Native children. Although the book is designed for educators, it can be equally valuable for students. C

684 McCullum, Hugh, and McCullum, Karmel. *This Land Is Not for Sale: Canada's Original People and Their Land; A Saga of Neglect, Exploitation, and Conflict.* Toronto: Anglican Book Centre, 1975, 210 pp., paper.

"This book is about Indian, Inuit, and Métis land claims and Northern development." D

685 *Métis and Native Uprisings and the Land Question* (kit). Toronto: NC Press, n.d. 4 filmstrips, 4 cassettes, 1 teacher's guide.

686 Mowat, William, and Mowat, Christine, eds. *Native Peoples in Canadian Literature.* Toronto: Macmillan, 1975, 122 pp., paper.

A literary anthology. B

687 "The Native Condition: A Canadian Tragedy." *Maclean's*, May 1973, p. 25.

This special section includes articles by George Manuel, Maria Campbell, and Duke Redbird.

688 *The Native People.* Semimonthly.

This newspaper provides coverage of Native news in Canada, with a major emphasis on Alberta.

689 *Nigger in a Parka* (audiotape). Toronto: Canadian Broadcasting Corporation, n.d. (60 min.)

The impact of the white man's search for wealth in the North on the way of life of the Native Peoples.

690 O'Malley, Martin. *The Past and Future Land: An Account of the Berger Inquiry into the Mackenzie Valley Pipeline.* Toronto: Peter Martin Associates, 1976, 280 pp., paper and cloth.

Testimonies before the Berger Inquiry, many of them from Indians and Inuit.

691 Patterson, Nancy-Lou. *Canadian Native Art: Arts and Crafts of Canadian Indians and Eskimos.* Toronto: Collier-Macmillan, 1973, 180 pp., cloth.

Well illustrated. D

692 *People of the Land: Northwest Territories* (audiotape). Toronto: Canadian Broadcasting Corporation, n.d. (30 min., reel and cassette)

The relationship between the physical geography of the North and the lifestyles found there.

693 Sanders, Douglas Esmond. *Native People in Areas of Internal National Expansion: Indians and Inuit in Canada.* Copenhagen: International Work Group for Indigenous Affairs, 1973, 39 pp., paper. Distributor: Latin American Working Group.

Sanders, a law professor, examines legal issues associated with the Native Peoples and development projects such as the Bennett Dam and the James Bay project. D

694 Sealey, D. Bruce, and Kirkness, Verna J., eds. *Indians without Tipis: A Resource Book by Indians and Métis.* 2d ed. Agincourt, Ont.: Book Society of Canada, 1974, paper.

This book includes the following topics: history of the Métis, native culture and contributions, problems and solutions, the native experience in urban areas, and a case study of an isolated northern community. C

695 *Tawow* (kit). Agincourt, Ont.: Book Society of Canada, n.d. 50 study cards, 100 photo cards, 1 filmstrip, 2 cassettes, 100 review cards, 1 teacher's guide, 4 introductory and general reference cards, 2 reference books for teachers, and resource material (1 book, 1 play, 1 essay) for students.

NORWEGIANS (See also Scandinavians)

696 Brunvand, Jan Harold. *Norwegian Settlers in Alberta.* Ottawa: National Museum of Man, Canadian Centre for Folk Culture Studies, 1974, 71 pp., paper.

A study of Norwegian folk culture in the Camrose area of Alberta. D

697 Kopas, C. R. *Bella Coola.* Vancouver: Mitchell Press, 1970, 295 pp., cloth.

A local history of Bella Coola, B.C. There are two chapters on Norwegian settlers. B

ORIENTALS (See also Chinese and Japanese)

698 Glynn-Ward, Hilda (pseud.). *The Writing on the Wall: Chinese and Japanese Immigration to B.C., 1920.* Introduction by Patricia Roy. Toronto: University of Toronto Press, 1974, 148 pp., paper.

The author uses the novel format to thinly disguise anti-Oriental immigration propaganda. Originally published in 1921. C

699 *Keeping British Columbia White: Anti-Orientalism in the Canadian West* (slides). Ottawa: National Film Board and National Museum of Man, n.d. 30 slides (color and black and white), 1 teacher's booklet. Distributor: Scholar's Choice.

700 Lee, Carol F. "The Road to Enfranchisement: Chinese and Japanese in British Columbia." *BC Studies*, no. 30, 1976, pp. 44-76. D

701 Lower, J. Arthur. *Canada on the Pacific Rim.* Toronto: McGraw-Hill Ryerson, 1975, 230 pp., paper and cloth.

Contains two chapters on Asian immigrants in Canada. C

702 ———. "'Official' Racism." *Canada and the World*, December 1977, pp. 16-17.

A history of Orientals and East Indians in British Columbia. B

703 Palmer, Howard D. "Anti-Oriental Sentiment in Alberta 1880-1920." *Canadian Ethnic Studies*, vol. 2, no. 2, 1970, pp. 31-58. D

704 Roy, Patricia E. "Educating the 'East': B.C. and the Oriental Question in the Interwar Years." *BC Studies*, no. 18, 1973, pp. 50-69. D

705 ———. "The Oriental 'Menace' in British Columbia." In *Studies in Canadian Social History*, pp. 287-97. Edited by M. Horn and R. Sabourin. Toronto: McClelland and Stewart, 1974, paper.

This paper examines attitudes towards Orientals in British Columbia during the 1920s. The views of various groups such as politicians, farmers, and merchants are explored. D

706 ———. "Protecting His Pocketbook and Preserving His Race: The White Merchant and Oriental Competition." In *Cities in the West*, pp. 243-58. Edited by A. R. McCormack and Ian MacPherson. Ottawa: National Museum of Man, 1972. D

707 Sugimoto, Howard H. "The Vancouver Riots of 1907: A Canadian Example." In *East across the Pacific: Historical and Sociological Studies of Japanese Immigration and Assimilation*, pp. 92-126. Edited by Hilary Conroy, and T. Scott Miyakawa. Santa Barbara, Calif.: American Bibiographical Centre-Clio Press, 1972, paper and cloth.

An excellent study of the anti-Oriental riots. D

708 Ward, W. Peter. "The Oriental Immigrant and Canada's Protestant Clergy, 1858-1925." *BC Studies*, no. 22, 1974, pp. 40-55. D

PAKISTANIS (See also South Asians)

709 Awan, Sadiq Noor Alam. *The People of Pakistani Origin in Canada: The First Quarter Century*. Ottawa: Canadian-Pakistan Association, 1976, 48 pp., paper. D

POLES

710 *Kaszuby* (motion picture). Montreal: National Film Board, 1975. (16mm, 28 min., color)

The Kaszubian Polish settlement at Barry's Bay, Ontario.

711 Krychowski, T. W., ed. *Polish Canadians: Profile and Image.* Toronto: Polish Canadian Research Institute, 1969, 111 pp., cloth.

Six papers with social science themes. E

712 Lee-Whiting, Brenda B. "First Polish Settlement in Canada." *Canadian Geographical Journal*, September 1967, pp. 108-12.

The history of Polish settlements in Wilno and Barry's Bay, Ontario, established in the years 1860-63. C

713 Radecki, Henry, and Heydenkorn, Benedykt. *A Member of a Distinguished Family: The Polish Group in Canada.* Toronto: McClelland and Stewart, 1976, 240 pp., paper and cloth.

A history. Part of the ethnic history series commissioned by the Department of the Secretary of State. D

714 "Renfrew County and the Polish Settlement." *Canadian Collector*, November/December 1975, pp. 14-16.

A history of Polish settlement in Renfrew County, Ontario. C

715 Turek, Victor. *Poles in Manitoba.* Toronto: Polish Canadian Research Institute, 1967, 339 pp., cloth.

A historical and sociological perspective. E

PORTUGUESE

716 Anderson, Grace M. *Networks of Contact: The Portuguese and Toronto.* Waterloo, Ont.: Wilfrid Laurier University Publications, 1974, 195 pp., paper and cloth.

A sociological study examining "networks of contact, or the importance of who the immigrant knows." About half of the chapters provide either background material or discussions of general topics related to the Portuguese. D

717 Anderson, Grace M., and Higgs, David. *A Future to Inherit: The Portuguese Communities of Canada.* Toronto: McClelland and Stewart, 1976, 202 pp., paper and cloth.

A sociological and historical perspective on the Portuguese community. Part of the ethnic history series sponsored by the Department of the Secretary of State. D

718 *Bibliography of Centre's Resources on the Portuguese in Toronto, and Related Materials.* Toronto: Cross-Cultural Communication Centre, 1977, 4 pp., mimeo, free.

719 Nankivell, Joan. "They Never Really Left Home." *Weekend Magazine*, 11 August 1973, p. 16.

A very good portrayal of the Portuguese immigrant experience in Canada. C

720 Ontario. Ministry of Culture and Recreation. Multicultural Development Branch. *Papers on the Portuguese Community.* Toronto: n.d., 18 pp., free.

Two papers on social and cultural change among the Portuguese. C

721 Peters, A. "The Portuguese Community—in Winnipeg." *Manitoba Modern Language Bulletin*, vol. 8, no. 2, 1974, pp. 12-18. C

SCANDINAVIANS (See also Danes, Finns, Icelanders, Norwegians, and Swedes)

722 Wonders, William C. "Scandinavian Homesteaders." *Alberta History*, vol. 24, no. 3, 1976, pp. 1-4.

A short history. D

SCOTS (See also British)

723 Campbell, Alphonsus P. "The Heritage of the Highland Scots in Prince Edward Island." *Revue de l'Université d'Ottawa*, vol. 44, no. 1, 1974, pp. 49-57.

A highly personal and very revealing account of the social and cultural characteristics of the Highland Scots. C

724 Campbell, D., and Maclean, R. A. *Beyond the Atlantic Roar: A Study of Nova Scotia Scots.* Toronto: McClelland and Stewart, 1974, 328 pp., paper.

A study of the Scots in eastern Nova Scotia using both the historical and sociological perspectives. D

725 Dunn, Charles W. *Highland Settler: A Portrait of the Scottish Gael in Nova Scotia.* Toronto: University of Toronto Press, 1953, paper and cloth.

A study using the folk culture perspective. D

726 Galbraith, John Kenneth. *The Scotch.* New York: New American Library, 1970, 145 pp., paper.

Galbraith reflects on the Scottish culture he knew as a child growing up in southern Ontario. D

727 Hill, Douglas. *Great Emigrations I: The Scots to Canada.* London: Gentry Books, 1972, 136 pp., cloth. Distributor: General Publishing.

A history of Scottish emigration to Canada until the mid-1800s. Considerable emphasis is placed on homeland conditions.

728 Reid, W. Stanford. "The Scot and Canadian Identity." *The Lakehead University Review*, vol. 4, no. 1, 1971, pp. 1-25.

The role Scots have played in moulding Canadian history and forming the Canadian identity. D

729 Reid, Stanford, ed. *The Scottish Tradition in Canada.* Toronto: McClelland and Stewart, 1976, 324 pp., paper and cloth.

A comprehensive scholarly history. Part of the ethnic history series sponsored by the Department of the Secretary of State. D

730 *The Scots* (motion picture or videocassette). Toronto: CTV Television, n.d. (16mm, or 3/4" videocassette, 50 min., color)

"A picture of proud, hard-working people who make up a large percentage of Canada's population and have contributed much to our heritage."

731 Sherwood, Roland H. "The Coming of the Scots: 200th Anniversary." *Atlantic Advocate*, April 1973, pp. 10-13.

The *Hector* brought Scottish settlers to Pictou, Nova Scotia in 1773. Their early experiences are described. C

732 Thomson, James, and Preston, Richard Arthur, eds. *For Friends at Home: A Scottish Emigrant's Letters from Canada, California, and the Cariboo 1844-1864.* Montreal: McGill-Queen's University Press, 1975, 352 pp., cloth.

SLOVAKS

733 Gellner, John, and Smerek, John. *The Czechs and Slovaks in Canada.* Toronto: University of Toronto Press, 1968, 172 pp., cloth.

Emphasizes European background, settlement in Canada, distinctive organizations, and present-day involvement in Canadian society. D

SOUTH ASIANS (See also East Indians and Pakistanis)

734 Chandra, Kananur V. *Racial Discrimination in Canada: Asian Minorities.* San Francisco: R and E Research Associates, 1973, 80 pp., cloth.

A research report based upon a study conducted in Montreal among Indians, Pakistanis, and Bangladeshis. D

735 Hardwick, Francis C., ed. *From Far Beyond the Western Horizon: Canadians from the Indian Sub-Continent.* Vancouver: Tantalus Research, 1974, 80 pp., paper.

A history of South Asians largely based on extracts from primary and secondary sources. Includes questions and activities. B

736 Lower, J. Arthur. *Canada on the Pacific Rim.* Toronto: McGraw-Hill Ryerson, 1975, 230 pp., paper and cloth.

Contains two chapters on Asian immigrants in Canada. C

SWEDES (See also Scandinavians)

737 Barton, H. Arnold, ed. *Letters from the Promised Land: Swedes in America 1840-1914.* Minneapolis: University of Minnesota Press, 1975, 344 pp., cloth.

Some of the letters and documents included in this volume were written by Swedish immigrants in Canada. C

738 Houser, George J. *The Swedish Community at Eriksdale, Manitoba.* Ottawa: National Museum of Man, Canadian Centre for Folk Culture Studies, 1976, 112 pp., paper.

A study of Swedish folk culture based on interviews with 38 informants. C

739 Howard, Irene. *Vancouver's Svenskar: A History of the Swedish Community in Vancouver.* Vancouver: Vancouver Historical Society, 1970, 127 pp., cloth.

A history of Swedish immigration to British Columbia and early history of the Swedes in that province. Many extracts from primary sources are included and much of the book is biographical. C

UKRAINIANS

740 Faryna, Natalka, ed. *Ukrainian Canadiana.* Edmonton: Ukrainian Women's Association of Canada, 1976, 96 pp., cloth.

Ukrainian folk arts. Outstanding color photographs. C

741 Forman, Joan. *Westward to Canaan.* Toronto: Holt, Rinehart and Winston, 1972, 40 pp., paper.

A play based on the early immigration of Ukrainians to the prairies. B

742 Gregorovich, Andrew. *Chronology of Ukrainian Canadian History.* Toronto: Ukrainian Canadian Committee, 1974, 64 pp., paper.

A history of Ukrainian Canadians largely based on extracts from primary and secondary sources. Includes questions and activities. B

743 Hardwick, F. C., ed. *To the Promised Land: Contributions of Ukrainian Immigrants and Their Descendants to Canadian Society.* Vancouver: Tantalus Research, 1973, 62 pp., paper.

Designed for classroom use. B

744 Hillen, Ernest. "*Bitaemo* to the Town of Dauphin, Manitoba." *Weekend Magazine*, 22 September 1973, pp. 1-4.

The annual National Ukrainian Festival. B

745 *I've Never Walked the Steppes* (motion picture). Directed by Jerry Krepakevich. Montreal: National Film Board, 1975. (16mm, 28 min., color)

The story of two generations of the Karasevich family in Winnipeg. The younger generation discuss their Ukrainian heritage and how they relate to it.

746 Kaye, Vladmir J. *Early Ukrainian Settlements in Canada, 1895-1900: Dr. Josef Oleskow's Role in the Settlement of the Canadian Northwest.* Toronto: University of Toronto Press, 1964, 420 pp., cloth. D

747 Keywan, Zonia, and Coles, Martin. *Greater Than Kings: Ukrainian Pioneer Settlement in Canada.* Montreal: Harvest House, 1977, 165 pp., cloth.

An interesting blending of original narrative, oral history, extracts from primary sources, and period and contemporary photographs. C

748 Kostash, Myrna. *All of Baba's Children.* Edmonton: Hurtig, 1977, 413 pp., cloth.

A personal analysis of Ukrainian history in Alberta. Kostash attacks the mythology associated with Ukrainian-Canadian history and reconstructs her own relationship with her heritage. D

749 ——. "Baba Was a Bohunk." *Saturday Night*, October 1976, pp. 33-38.

The author explores her personal ethnic heritage and, in doing so, raises some important questions about ethnicity in Canada today. D

750 *Kurelek* (motion picture). Directed by William Pettigrew. Montreal: National Film Board, 1966. (16mm and 35mm, 10 min., color)

Artist William Kurelek's portrayal of immigrant homesteaders and the Ukraine, his father's homeland.

751 Lehr, John C. "Changing Ukrainian

751 Lehr, John C. "Changing Ukrainian House Styles." *Alberta History*, vol. 23, no. 1, 1975, pp. 25-29.

752 MacGregor, J. G. *Vilni Zemli (Free Lands): The Ukrainian Settlement of Alberta.* Toronto: McClelland and Stewart, 1969, 274 pp., cloth.

A history of early Ukrainian immigration and settlement in Alberta. The experiences of the early settlers are stressed. C

753 Potrebenko, Helen. *No Streets of Gold: A Social History of Ukrainians in Alberta.* Vancouver: New Star Books, 1977, 311 pp., paper and cloth. D

754 *The Ukrainian Canadian.* Monthly.

Contains a variety of articles on Ukrainian-Canadian history and culture.

755 *The Ukrainians—Canadian Homesteaders: Strangers to Canada* and *Prairie Homestead* (kit). Scarborough: ETHOS, 1975. 2 filmstrips, 1 cassette, 1 teacher's manual, and reading script.

Prepared for secondary school students.

756 Woycenko, Ol'ha. *The Ukrainians in Canada.* Rev. ed. Winnipeg: Trident Press, 1968, 271 pp., cloth.

A history of Ukrainian immigration, settlement, and society. Emphasis is placed on the outstanding accomplishments and achievements of individual Ukrainians. C

VIETNAMESE

757 Cobb, David. "Battle Lines on Bleury Street." *Canadian Magazine*, 30 March 1974, pp. 20-22.

Montreal's Vietnamese community and the divisions within it based on political aspirations for the homeland. B

758 "Immigration: Fitting In." *Time*, 28 July 1975, pp. 9-10.

Vietnamese refugees in Canada. C

759 McDonald, Marci. "Orphans of the Storm." *Maclean's*, 8 March 1976, p. 26.

Vietnamese refugees in Montreal. C

760 *The Sometime Samaritan* (motion picture or videocassette). Toronto: CTV Television, n.d. (16mm, or 3/4" videocassette, 25 min., color)

Vietnamese refugees in Canada. One program in the "Maclear" series.

WELSH (See also British)

761 Thomas, Lewis H. "From the Pampas to the Prairies: The Welsh Migration of 1902." *Saskatchewan History*, vol. 24, no. 1, 1971, pp. 1-12.

A Welsh community first settled in Patagonia, Argentina, then later moved to Saskatchewan.

WEST INDIANS (See also Blacks)

762 *Bibliography of Centre's Resources on the West Indian/Black Communities in Canada and Toronto and Related Materials.* Toronto: Cross-Cultural Communication Centre, 7 pp., mimeo, free.

763 Blizzard, Flora Helena. *West Indians in Canada: A Selective Annotated Bibliography.* Guelph, Ont.: University of Guelph Library, 1970, 41 pp., paper.

764 *Contrast.* Weekly.

Contrast is primarily oriented to Toronto's West Indian community.

765 Diebel, Linda. "Black Women in White Canada: The Lonely Life." *Chatelaine*, March 1973, p. 38.

West Indian immigrants. C

766 Itwaru, Arnold H. "A New Society: Transition of the Immigrant." *Spear*, June 1977, pp. 32-35.

The West Indian immigrant experience. C

Addresses

Allyn and Bacon Canada
791 St. Clair Avenue West
Toronto, Ontario
M6C 1B8

American Bibliographical Centre-Clio Press
Riviera Campus
2040 Alameda Padre Serra
Santa Barbara, California
93103

The Anglican Book Centre
600 Jarvis Street
Toronto, Ontario
M4Y 2J6

Atheneum
order from McClelland and Stewart

Bantam Books of Canada
60 St. Clair Avenue East
Toronto, Ontario
M4T 1N5

Bell Books
612 Herald Building
206 – 7 Avenue Southwest
Calgary, Alberta
T2P 0N7

Book Society of Canada
P. O. Box 200
Agincourt, Ontario
M1S 3B6

Brunswick Press
360 King Street
Fredericton, New Brunswick
E3B 5A2

Burns and MacEachern
62 Railside Road
Don Mills, Ontario
M3A 1A6

Butterworth
2265 Midland Avenue
Scarborough, Ontario
M1P 4S1

C.A.S.N.P. Bulletin
see Canadian Association in Support of the Native Peoples

CTV Television
Educational Film Distribution
42 Charles Street East
Toronto, Ontario
M4Y 1T5

Canadian Association in Support of the Native Peoples
251 Laurier Avenue West
Ottawa, Ontario
K1P 5J6

Canadian Broadcasting Corporation
P. O. Box 500, Station A
Toronto, Ontario
M5W 1E6

Canadian Consultative Council on Multiculturalism
Multiculturalism Directorate
Department of the Secretary of State
66 Slater Street
Ottawa, Ontario
K1A 0M5

Canadian Council for International Cooperation
75 Sparks Street
Ottawa, Ontario
K1P 5A5

Canadian Ethnic Studies
The University of Calgary
Calgary, Alberta
T2N 1N4

Canadian Historical Association
c/o Public Archives
395 Wellington Street
Ottawa, Ontario
K1A 0N3

The Canadian India Times
161 Dalhousie Street
Ottawa, Ontario

Canadian Labour Congress
2841 Riverside Drive
Ottawa, Ontario
K1V 8X7

Canadian-Pakistan Association
P. O. Box 558, Station B
Ottawa, Ontario
K1P 5P6

Centennial Publications
600 Shaftesbury Boulevard
Winnipeg, Manitoba

Clarke Irwin
791 St. Clair Avenue West
Toronto, Ontario
M6C 1B8

Coles Publishing
910 Ronson Drive
Rexdale, Ontario
M9W 1C1

Collier-Macmillan
1125B Leslie Street
Don Mills, Ontario
M3C 2K2

Commcept Publishing
470 Granville Street
Vancouver, British Columbia
V6C 1V5

Comprint Publishing
P. O. Box 4642, Station C
Calgary, Alberta

Conference of Mennonites in Canada
600 Shaftesbury Boulevard
Winnipeg, Manitoba
R3P 0M4

Conrad Press
Conrad Grebel College
Waterloo, Ontario
N2L 3G6

Contrast
28 Lennox Street
Toronto, Ontario

Copp Clark Publishing
517 Wellington Street West
Toronto, Ontario
M5V 1G1

Cross-Cultural Communication Centre
1991 Dufferin Street
Toronto, Ontario
M6E 3P9

Dalhousie University Press
Dalhousie University
Halifax, Nova Scotia
B3H 3J5

J. M. Dent and Sons (Canada)
100 Scarsdale Road
Don Mills, Ontario
M3B 2R8

Department of Indian and Northern Affairs
Information Services
400 Laurier Avenue West
Ottawa, Ontario
K1A 0H4

Department of Labour
see Labour Canada

Department of Manpower and Immigration
see Employment and Immigration Canada

Department of Northern Affairs and Natural Resources
see Department of Indian and Northern Affairs

Department of the Secretary of State
Information Services
66 Slater Street
Ottawa, Ontario
K1A 0M5

Doubleday Publishers
105 Bond Street
Toronto, Ontario
M5B 1Y3

J. J. Douglas Publishing
1875 Welsh Street
North Vancouver, British Columbia
V7P 1B7

ERIC Clearing House for Social Studies/Social Science Education
see Social Science Education Consortium

ETHOS
Unit 9, 2250 Midland Avenue
Scarborough, Ontario
M1P 3E6

Employment and Immigration Canada
Information Services
305 Rideau Street
Ottawa, Ontario
K1A 0J9

Fitzhenry and Whiteside
150 Lesmill Road
Don Mills, Ontario
M3B 2T5

Freeman Publishing
P. O. Box 1673
Saskatoon, Saskatchewan

Gage Publishing
P. O. Box 5000
164 Commander Boulevard
Agincourt, Ontario
M1S 3C7

General Publishing
30 Lesmill Road
Don Mills, Ontario
M3B 2T6

Glenbow-Alberta Institute
9 Avenue and 1 Street Southeast
Calgary, Alberta

Government of Ontario Bookstore
880 Bay Street
Toronto, Ontario

Gray's Publishing
P. O. Box 2160
Sidney, British Columbia
V8L 3S6

Griffin House Publishers
461 King Street West
Toronto, Ontario
M5V 1K7

Hamilton Anti-Racism Committee
35 Catherine Street South
Hamilton, Ontario

Hancock House
3215 Island View Road
Saanichton, British Columbia
V0S 1M0

Harvard University Press
order from Book Centre
1140 Beaulac Street
Montreal, Quebec
H4R 1R8

Harvest House
4795 St. Catherine Street West
Montreal, Quebec
H3Z 2B9

Heritage
Alberta Culture
11th Floor – CN Tower
Edmonton, Alberta
T5J 0K5

Historical Society of Alberta
P. O. Box 4035, Station C
Calgary, Alberta
T2T 5M9

Historical Society of Mecklenburg Upper Canada
P. O. Box 406, Station K
Toronto, Ontario
M4P 2G7

Holt, Rinehart and Winston of Canada
55 Horner Avenue
Toronto, Ontario
M8Z 4X6

Houghton Mifflin Canada
Unit A, 67 Steelcase Road
Markham, Ontario
M2H 2W2

Hurtig Publishers
10560 105 Street
Edmonton, Alberta
T2H 2W7

The Icelandic Canadian
c/o Harold Johnson
868 Arlington Street
Winnipeg, Manitoba
R3E 2E4

Imperial Oil Limited
Public Affairs Department
111 St. Clair Avenue West
Toronto, Ontario
M5W 1K3

Indian News
see Department of Indian and Northern Affairs

Information Canada
see Supply and Services Canada

International Tele-Film Enterprises
47 Densley Avenue
Toronto, Ontario
M6M 5A8

Inuit Cultural Institute
Eskimo Point, Northwest Territories
X0C 0E0

Inuit Tapirisat of Canada
222 Somerset Street West
Ottawa, Ontario
K2P 2G3

Inuit Today
see Inuit Tapirisat of Canada

Irwin-Dorsey
265 Guelph Street
Georgetown, Ontario
17G 4B3

Jewish Historical Society of Canada Journal
c/o Rabbi Dr. J. V. Plaut
Congregation Beth El
2525 Mark Avenue
Windsor, Ontario
N9E 2W2

Johns Hopkins University Press
order from Burns and MacEachern

Kootenay Doukhobor Historical Society/
Continneh Books
P. O. Box 3024
Castlegar, British Columbia
V1N 3H4

Labour Canada
Information Services
Ottawa, Ontario
K1A 0J2

Latin American Working Group
P. O. Box 6300, Station A
Toronto, Ontario

Learnxs Press
155 College Street
Toronto, Ontario
M5T 1P6

J. M. LeBel Enterprises
10624 84 Avenue
Edmonton, Alberta
T6E 2H6

James Lewis and Samuel
see James Lorimer

Longman Canada
55 Barber Greene Road
Don Mills, Ontario
M3C 2A1

James Lorimer
35 Britain Street
Toronto, Ontario
M5A 1R7

Maclean-Hunter Learning Materials
70 Bond Street
Toronto, Ontario
M5B 1X3

McClelland and Stewart
25 Hollinger Road
Toronto, Ontario
M4B 3G2

McClelland and Stewart West
see McClelland and Stewart

McGill–Queen's University Press
Purvis Hall
1020 Pine Avenue West
Montreal, Quebec
H3A 1A2

McGraw-Hill Ryerson
330 Progress Avenue
Scarborough, Ontario
M1P 2Z5

K. A. McLeod
Faculty of Education
University of Toronto
371 Bloor Street West
Toronto, Ontario
M5S 2R7

Macmillan of Canada
70 Bond Street
Toronto, Ontario
M5B 1X3

Manitoba Métis Federation Press
301 374 Donald Street
Winnipeg, Manitoba

Peter Martin Associates
35 Britain Street
Toronto, Ontario
M5A 1R7

Mennonite Historian
600 Shaftesbury Boulevard
Winnipeg, Manitoba
R3P 0M4

Mennonite Historical Society of Ontario
Conrad Grebel College
University of Waterloo
Waterloo, Ontario

Methuen Publications
2330 Midland Avenue
Agincourt, Ontario
M1S 1P7

Métis Association of the Northwest Territories
P. O. Box 1375
Yellowknie
Yellowknife, Northwest Territories
X0E 1H0

Mika Publishing
P. O. Box 536
200 Stanley Street
Belleville, Ontario
K8N 5B2

Ministry of Culture and Recreation
Multicultural Development Branch
77 Bloor Street West
Toronto, Ontario
M7A 2R9

Ministry of Government Services
Printing Services Branch
Parliament Buildings
Toronto, Ontario
M7A 1N5

Ministry of Labour
Research Branch
400 University Avenue
Toronto, Ontario
M7A 1T7

Mir Publishing
P. O. Box 730
Grand Forks, British Columbia
V0H 1H0

Mitchell Press
P. O. Box 6000
Vancouver, British Columbia
V6B 4B9

Moreland-Latchford Productions
229 Queen Street West
Toronto, Ontario
M5V 2S6

Multiculturalism
Faculty of Education
University of Toronto
371 Bloor Street West
Toronto, Ontario
M5S 2R7

Multi News
see Department of the Secretary of State

NC Press
P. O. Box 4010, Terminal A
Toronto, Ontario
M5W 1H8

National Council for the Social Studies
1515 Wilson Boulevard
Arlington, Virginia

National Film Board
P. O. Box 6100
Montreal, Quebec
H3C 3H5

National Indian Brotherhood
102 Bank Street
Ottawa, Ontario
K1P 5N4

National Museum of Man
Publications Distribution and Sales
300 Laurier Avenue West
Ottawa, Ontario
K1A 0M8

National Museum of Man
Canadian Centre for Folk Culture Studies
Ottawa, Ontario
K1A 0M8

The Native Peoples
9311 60 Avenue
Edmonton, Alberta

Thomas Nelson and Sons (Canada)
81 Curlew Drive
Don Mills, Ontario
M3A 2R1

New American Library of Canada
100 Steelcase Road East
Markham, Ontario
L3R 1E8

The New Canadian
479 Queen Street West
Toronto, Ontario
M5V 2A9

New Press
30 Lesmill Road
Don Mills, Ontario
M3B 2T6

New Star Books
2504 York Avenue
Vancouver, British Columbia
V6K 1E3

North American Indian Films
529 Sussex Drive
Ottawa, Ontario
K1N 6Z6

Northern Mosaic
P. O. Box 2334, Station B
Thunder Bay, Ontario

Ontario Human Rights Commission
400 University Avenue
Toronto, Ontario
M7A 1T7

Ontario Institute for Studies in Education
Publications Sales
252 Bloor Street West
Toronto, Ontario
M5S 1V6

Oxford University Press
70 Wynford Drive
Don Mills, Ontario
M3C 1J9

Paperjacks
25 Torbay Road
Markham, Ontario
L3R 1H1

Peguis Publishers
462 Hargrave Street
Winnipeg, Manitoba
R3A 0X5

Penguin Books of Canada
41 Steelcase Road West
Markham, Ontario
L3R 1B4

Polish Canadian Research Institute
288 Roncesvalles Avenue
Toronto, Ontario
M6R 2M4

Prentice-Hall of Canada
1870 Birchmount Road
Scarborough, Ontario
M1P 2J7

Provincial Archives of British Columbia
Aural History Division
Victoria, British Columbia

Quill and Quire
59 Front Street East
Toronto, Ontario
M5E 1B3

R and E Research Associates
4843 Mission Street
San Francisco, California
94112

Random House
5390 Ambler Drive
Mississauga, Ontario
L4W 1Y7

Reader's Digest Association
215 Redfern Avenue
Montreal, Quebec
H3Z 2V9

Rikka
P. O. Box 6031, Station A
Toronto, Ontario
M5W 1P4

Samuel Steven Publishers
554 Spadina Crescent
Toronto, Ontario
M5F 2J9

Scholar's Choice
50 Ballantyne Avenue
Stratford, Ontario
N5A 6T9

Simon and Schuster of Canada
330 Steelcase Road
Markham, Ontario
L3R 2M1

Social Science Education Consortium
855 Broadway
Boulder, Colorado
80302

Supply and Services Canada
Printing and Publishing
270 Albert Street
Ottawa, Ontario
K1A 0S9

Tantalus Research
P. O. Box 34248
2405 Pine Street
Vancouver, British Columbia
V6J 4N8

Thunder Bay Finnish-Canadian Historical Society
314 Bay Street
Thunder Bay, Ontario

Trident Press
P. O. Box 3629, Station B
Winnipeg, Mait
Winnipeg, Manitoba
R2W 3R4

Tundra Books
1374 Sherbrooke Street West
Montreal, Quebec
H3G 1J6

The Ukrainian Canadian
1164 Dundas Street West
Toronto, Ontario
M6J 1X4

Ukrainian Canadian Committee
191 Lippincott Street
Toronto, Ontario
M5S 2P3

Ukrainian Women's Association of Canada
St. John's Ladies Auxiliary
10611 110 Avenue
Edmonton, Alberta

University of British Columbia Bookstore
2075 Wesbrook Place
Vancouver, British Columbia
V6T 1W5

University of Chicago Press
11030 South Langley Avenue
Chicago, Illinois
60628

University of Guelph Library
Guelph, Ontario
N1H 6N5

University of Minnesota Press
order from Burns and MacEachern

University of Regina
Canadian Plains Research Centre
Regina, Saskatchewan
S4S 0A2

University of Saskatchewan Bookstore
Saskatoon, Saskatchewan
S7N 0W0

University of Toronto
Faculty of Education
Guidance Centre
1000 Yonge Street
Toronto, Ontario
M4W 2K8

University of Toronto Press
5201 Dufferin Street
Downsview, Ontario
M3H 5T8

University of Winnipeg Press
Winnipeg, Manitoba
R3B 2E9

Vancouver Historical Society
P. O. Box 3071
Vancouver, British Columbia

Van Nostrand and Reinhold
1410 Birchmount Road
Scarborough, Ontario
M1P 2E7

Western Extension College
804 Central Avenue
Saskatoon, Saskatchewan
S7N 2G6

Western Publishers
P. O. Box 30193, Station B
Calgary, Alberta

John Wiley and Sons
22 Worcester Road
Rexdale, Ontario
M9W 1L1

Wilfrid Laurier University Press
Centre Hall, Wilfrid Laurier University
Waterloo, Ontario
N2L 3C5

OTHER OISE PUBLICATIONS
ON CULTURAL ISSUES

Issues in Cultural Diversity
Harold Troper and Lee Palmer

A study unit for secondary school students intended to stimulate discussion and reflection on the question of cultural minorities. Case studies focus on individual versus collective "rights," the preservation of culturally distinctive neighbourhoods, housing and discrimination, intergroup tensions, employment, and government immigration policies. 130 pages, 1976.

Native Survival
John Eisenberg and Harold Troper

A study unit for secondary school students that is intended to stimulate discussion and reflection on the place of native peoples in Canadian society. Case studies encourage consideration of such issues as the intrusion of white society, the question of special status or equality, and the education of children from reserves. 104 pages, 1973.

Debates about Canada's Future: 1868-1896
Virginia Robeson, editor

Excerpts from original sources concerning Canada's role and identity as a newly emerging nation. Of central concern are minority rights and French-English relations. Suitable for use in Canadian studies courses for senior-level students. 116 pages, 1977.

What Culture? What Heritage?
A. B. Hodgetts

An investigation of curriculum content and teaching across Canada in the '60s, in which the author denounces existing approaches to Canadian history and social studies, and lays in the groundwork for future change. 122 pages, 1968.

Teaching Canada for the '80s
A. B. Hodgetts and Paul Gallegher

A carefully wrought series of concrete proposals for the teaching of Canada studies from elementary through secondary school. The authors provide a framework for Canada studies touching all curriculum areas that is "pan-Canadian" in objective, yet that emphasizes the pluralism and diversity of Canada and the Canadian people. 136 pages, 1978.

The Education of Immigrant Students: Issues and Answers
Aaron Wolfgang, editor

Sixteen collected papers focussing on approaches and goals in teaching recent immigrants. The contributors examine some successful programs, the implications of recent research into language and cultural problems, ways in which current approaches might be improved, and the question of ethnic pluralism. 274 pages, 1975.

Teaching Prejudice

Garnet McDiarmid and David Pratt

Recommendations arising from an investigation of the treatment of minority groups in social studies texts widely used the early '70s. The authors also describe analytical techniques that teachers and students can apply to both written and pictorial material from other sources. 129 pages, 1971.

Caribbean Canadians

A two-tape series that considers the problems of immigrants from the Caribbean in adjusting to Canadian society. Tapes may be purchased separately or together.

Becoming Canadian. Joan Browne (Institute for Public Affairs, Dalhousie University, and president of the Nova Scotia Association for Colored Peoples) details the problems of recent Caribbean immigrants in smaller cities and in relation to native Canadian blacks. Rosemary Brown (a British Columbia M.L.A. and social worker) talks about West Indian multiculturalism in the Canadian mosaic, and the culture shock of becoming part of this mosaic. 60 minutes, 1977.

Adapting to the Metropolis. Austin Clarke (the noted author, reporter, and professor of literature) and Hank Clarke (teacher, member of the Black Education Project, and contributor to a report on racism and education) discuss adjusting to big-city living, the Caribbean immigrant as a typical immigrant, the school in relation to immigrant problems, and the needs of the family in fitting into society. 60 minutes, 1977.

Prices and a complete list of current OISE publications may be obtained from Publications Sales, The Ontario Institute for Studies in Education, 252 Bloor Street West, Toronto, Ontario M5S 1V6.